A WOMAN OF NO IMPORTANCE

OSCAR WILDE

NOTES BY FRANCES GRAY

 Longman

York Press

The right of Frances Gray to be identified as Author
of this Work has been asserted by her in accordance
with the Copyright, Designs and Patents Act 1988

YORK PRESS
322 Old Brompton Road, London SW5 9JH

PEARSON EDUCATION LIMITED
Edinburgh Gate, Harlow,
Essex CM20 2JE, United Kingdom
Associated companies, branches and representatives throughout the world

Quotations from *A Woman of No Importance* by Oscar Wilde are from the New
Mermaids edition of the play published by A & C Black (second edition, 1993
reprinted 2006)

First published 2007
Second impression 2008

ISBN 978–1–4058–6179–3

Phototypeset by utimestwo, Northamptonshire
Printed in China

PART ONE

INTRODUCTION

HOW TO STUDY A PLAY

Studying on your own requires self-discipline and a carefully thought-out work plan in order to be effective.

- Drama is a special kind of writing (the technical term is 'genre') because it needs a performance in the theatre to arrive at a full interpretation of its meaning. Try to imagine that you are a member of the audience when reading the play. Think about how it could be presented on the stage, not just about the words on the page.

- Drama is always about conflict of some sort (which may be below the surface). Identify the conflicts in the play and you will be close to identifying the large ideas or themes which bind all the parts together.

- Make careful notes on themes, character, plot and any subplots of the play.

- Why do you like or dislike the characters in the play? How do your feelings towards them develop and change?

- Playwrights find non-realistic ways of allowing an audience to see into the minds and motives of their characters, for example through an **aside** or music. Consider how such dramatic devices are used in the play you are studying.

- Think of the playwright writing the play. Why were these particular arrangements of events, characters and speeches chosen?

- Cite exact sources for all quotations, whether from the text itself or from critical commentaries. Wherever possible find your own examples from the play to back up your opinions.

- Where appropriate, comment in detail on the language of the passage you have quoted.

- Always express your ideas in your own words.

These York Notes offer an introduction to *A Woman of No Importance* and cannot substitute for close reading of the text and the study of secondary sources.

CHECK THE BOOK
Ronald Hayman's *How to Read a Play* (1977, revised and updated 1999) is an excellent introduction to the study of drama.

READING *A WOMAN OF NO IMPORTANCE*

CHECK THE BOOK

Sheridan Morley's *Oscar Wilde* (1976) is a short and entertaining biography and an exceptionally good visual resource, including photographs of Wilde's first cast, designs, publicity material and sketches relating to the original production.

CHECK THE BOOK

H. Montgomery Hyde's *The Trials of Oscar Wilde*, published in 1948 for the Notable British Trials Series, offers a vivid insight into the attitude of the period towards homosexuals.

A Woman of No Importance advertised itself as a 'A new and original play of modern life.' The first night on 19 April 1893 at the most glamorous venue in London, the Theatre Royal, Haymarket, drew applause from a glittering audience – and boos. Oscar Wilde was part of the spectacle, bowing from a box and informing bemused spectators that 'Unfortunately Mr Oscar Wilde is not in the house.'

The reviews were as mixed as the reception. Everyone admired the sparkling wit, but Wilde was also accused of lacking seriousness. However, nobody agreed what he ought to be serious about. Some felt the plot was old-fashioned. Some felt it resembled the social-problem plays staged by experimental theatres rather than the West End. Others complained that there was no action and characters simply sat around smoking. Some dwelt on the personality of Wilde himself. He had already embarked on the tempestuous affair with Lord Alfred Douglas that landed him in prison two years later. He was blackmailed while the play was in rehearsal, and his reputation certainly coloured some responses to his work.

This concentration on single aspects tends to obscure the fact that the play does exactly what the playbill promised: it was new, original and modern in the 1890s and it remains provocative today. The originality lies in the combination of its elements. The plot was not new; the theatre of the 1890s was full of plays about 'fallen' women. They derived from French **boulevard dramas**, sophisticated plays about sexual secrets, watered down for an English theatre with the toughest censorship in Europe. Wilde transformed these stock situations by presenting them as comic in several senses of the term.

Comedy denotes above all a story with a happy ending; to allow a 'fallen' woman to achieve happiness – even, literally, to let her have the last word as Wilde does – would in itself have seemed slightly subversive to the Victorians. But the play is also a **comedy of manners**. Playwrights of the Restoration and eighteenth century who pioneered this genre used it to explore courtship, marriage and gender. They were noted for sparkling battles of wit between the sexes – but beneath the surface there was a strain of sadness. They could not escape the period's anxiety about sexual inequalities that made love, marriage or casual sex risky for both parties. Wilde's characters too live in a tightly organised society which discourages displays of feeling or frank statements of desire. However, wit and jokes provide them with a code through which they can express these. While we laugh, we also come to understand the social and sexual tensions beneath the surface.

When Wilde's characters seem to be most artificial, they are often at their most serious. Like Wilde himself, they are preoccupied with the business of self-presentation. Conventional Victorian wisdom saw 'character' as something unchangeable: you were born with certain traits and expressed them through your whole life. Wilde's stage figures invent and reinvent themselves. They construct their personalities through the language they use, the jokes they tell and the clothes they wear, rather like rock stars. Though their problems belong to another age, Wilde's characters do not seem dated. The most poised and witty figures in *A Woman of No Importance* are those comfortable with the idea of wearing a mask: they know that masks can still tell the truth. Hence some of the most apparently frothy **epigrams** are charged with biting social comment; it is the most cynical character who calls the condition of the London poor 'slavery' (Act I, p. 18).

Conventional Victorian dramas of love and marriage make a clear distinction between 'artificial' characters, who lie and deceive, and 'sincere' characters, who are honest and virtuous. However, even the most earnest characters in Wilde's play borrow language and literary stereotypes to express their needs and their feelings. Mrs Arbuthnot (the 'woman of no importance') lives in relative comfort – but when she speaks of looking after her illegitimate child 'Night and day all that long winter' (Act IV, p. 98), she sounds, quite unconsciously, like a **stock character** from popular **melodramas**. The fact that she adopts the language of these simple plays about village maidens and wicked squires reveals something about her view of her own actions. By the end of the play she can envisage a

CHECK THE BOOK

Katharine Worth's *Oscar Wilde* (1983) makes a case for *A Woman of No Importance* as one of Wilde's most original and experimental works for the stage, and explores the play's relationship with both **naturalism** and melodrama.

new future for herself; she stops speaking in **clichés** because she has greater awareness of her own individuality.

Wilde remarked in the *St James's Gazette* in 1895 that he admired the way English actors performed 'between the lines … capable of producing a wonderful dramatic effect by the aid of a monosyllable and two cigarettes'. He was one of the first to explore this talent. The play contains many moments where nothing is stated, but a great deal is implied by casual remarks or simple actions. A character walks out of the room and the audience is aware of emotional struggle; an aristocratic old lady shows what she feels about a fiercely political young woman with a request for 'my cotton that is just behind you' (Act II, p. 46).

In 1887 Wilde took on the editorship of a magazine called the *Lady's World*. His first act was to change the title to the *Woman's World* and add pieces on women's suffrage, feminism and literature to the articles on clothes. This preoccupation with the situation of women pervades *A Woman of No Importance*. As the title suggests, it explores their status in the world, their 'importance'. In an apparently relaxed setting, a country-house party, we see a group of figures with the power to shape the values and conduct of their world.

The male members of this group hold sway by rights legally invested in them by their country: they represent the aristocracy, the Church and Parliament. Effectively they are responsible for the fate of women. However, the female members have a more complex relationship to power. With few legal rights, they still exercise forms of social control. Some are bullies or nagging wives; others resort to emotional blackmail: 'The tyranny of the weak over the strong' (Act III, p. 69). The play shows these as figures of fun, caricatures that are a joy to watch; but there is an underlying political comment. Inequality ultimately damages the powerful as well as corrupting the weak. Other female characters manipulate men through their sexuality, discreetly flouting rules about relationships that exist to protect male interests. Wilde allows them to speak intimately and at length about their lack of freedom. They do so with a sparkling sophistication and remarkable frankness, pointing up the absurdity of treating intelligent women as children without rights.

CHECK THE BOOK

For more information about Wilde's time as editor of the *Woman's World*, Laurel Brake's *Subjugated Knowledges: Journalism, Gender and Literature, 1837–1907* (1994) is an interesting read.

CHECK THE BOOK

Mary Poovey's *Uneven Developments: The Ideological Work of Gender in Mid-Victorian England* (1988) deals with key aspects of legislation about marriage, divorce, property and rights affecting the lives of women throughout the period.

Concentrating as it does upon a social occasion rather than the sphere of work, the play could be said to focus on the world of women. In their different ways, however, the women in this privileged world seem to feel obligated to reinforce male dominance. Even those who most resent it pay lip service to the 'rules' about sexual behaviour. Hence they all ensure that theirs is a world full of secrets and private codes. They speak in discreetly veiled hints, and gossip about those who manage to stay within the boundaries of respectability. The gossip is entertaining but also cruel; we never lose sight of the fact that this world is merciless to those who venture too publicly beyond the boundaries. Inevitably, the plot becomes focused on an outsider who has done just that.

Wilde treats the situation in a remarkably modern style. All the attitudes traditionally employed in plays about 'fallen' women are there, but they are mocked and subverted. Conventional Victorian drama encouraged the audience to feel sentimental about the single mother or the repentant adulteress. However, it did not suggest that society should think differently about sexuality and the rights of women. Wilde's play leaves us with a series of questions: what should a 'fallen' woman do with the rest of her life? Is legal marriage so important that she should marry at the cost of her integrity? Should she repent a 'sin' that results in a beloved child? Are the rights of a father more important than those of a mother?

All plays involve conflicts. *A Woman of No Importance* has many. There are conflicts between characters: a mother and father battle over their son, and a pair of lovers struggle with their feelings. There are also wider conflicts: between the sexes, between the classes, between America and Europe, between **dandies** who value style and puritans who value truth. And there are conflicts of wit where all that matters is laughter. What makes all these conflicts so stimulating to watch is that they are never simplified. 'Good' characters are not necessarily likeable; 'bad' characters are entertaining even when they are at their least admirable. Sometimes the dandy speaks like a puritan, and the puritan tries on the stance of the dandy. And as the masks clash and the action unfolds, they always keep us guessing.

CHECK THE BOOK

Sos Eltis' *Revising Wilde: Society and Subversion in the Plays of Oscar Wilde* (1996) suggests that Wilde uses established conventions to mask views that the British theatre continued to censor until well into the next century.

PART TWO

THE TEXT

CHECK THE BOOK

Hesketh Pearson's *Beerbohm Tree: His Life and Laughter* (1956) gives an account of the relationship between Wilde and his leading man as they discussed and altered the text.

CHECK THE BOOK

Merlin Holland's *Complete Works of Oscar Wilde* (1994) is an authoritative edition that uses material available only to the Wilde family. It provides an insight into Wilde's working methods with two versions of *The Importance of Being Earnest,* and includes the complete text of *De Profundis.* Page numbers for Wilde's essays and plays other than *A Woman of No Importance* quoted in these Notes refer to the fifth edition of this *Complete Works*, published in 2003.

NOTE ON THE TEXT

The edition used in these Notes is the New Mermaids second edition, edited by Ian Small (1993, reprinted most recently in 2006).

A Woman of No Importance went through more drafts than any other play by Wilde. The New Mermaids second edition documents Wilde's own changes to the text (including name changes for the characters of Hester and Lord Illingworth); the cuts demanded by the Lord Chamberlain; the changes made prior to its performance by Sir Herbert Beerbohm Tree to make his role more sympathetic; and those made as a result of the audience's reaction to some lines, including some of the more radical political statements. The New Mermaids text adheres to the first edition of the play published by John Lane in 1894, probably prepared for publication by Wilde himself, in which he restored some of the material deleted for performance.

SYNOPSIS

The play opens on the lawn of Lady Hunstanton's house, where guests are relaxing. Hester, a young American, shows enthusiasm about a young bank clerk, Gerald Arbuthnot. He arrives with news: he has been offered a post as secretary to the rich and influential Lord Illingworth. Lady Hunstanton is delighted and writes inviting Gerald's mother to dinner. Other guests are introduced – two incorrigible flirts, Mrs Allonby and Lady Stutfield; the MP Mr Kelvil, who specialises in writing about 'Purity'; and the witty Lord Illingworth.

When Illingworth and Mrs Allonby are alone they flirt, and she throws out a challenge: to succeed with her, he must kiss Hester. Lord Illingworth catches sight of Mrs Arbuthnot's reply to Lady Hunstanton's dinner invitation and says the handwriting reminds him of someone he once knew – 'A woman of no importance' (Act I, p. 32).

As Act II begins, the women are discussing men and marriage. Mrs Allonby wittily outlines her image of the 'Ideal Man'. Hester is shocked by the conversation and disparages the English aristocracy, saying that men as well as women should be ostracised for sexual sin. Mrs Arbuthnot enters in time to hear this. They discuss Lord Illingworth, and Mrs Arbuthnot suddenly says she must see her son, Gerald.

When Gerald arrives his mother demands to leave. He insists she meet Lord Illingworth, and Mrs Arbuthnot and Illingworth talk alone. We learn that they had a youthful affair; she became pregnant with Gerald and left when Illingworth refused to marry her. They quarrel over their son; Mrs Arbuthnot does not want Illingworth to take Gerald away from her. As Gerald returns, Lord Illingworth challenges Mrs Arbuthnot to say why she does not want Gerald to work for him. His meaning – that if she refuses to allow it he will tell Gerald he was born out of wedlock – is clear. Mrs Arbuthnot gives in as the curtain falls.

In Act III Lord Illingworth begins to charm Gerald and gives advice on women and society. As the guests assemble, the conversation turns to the subject of forgiveness. Mrs Arbuthnot says that there is one thing a woman cannot forgive – the ruin of another woman's life. With the early departure of one of the guests, the Archdeacon, Dr Daubeny, the company breaks up for the evening. Hester seeks out Mrs Arbuthnot, feeling that they share a moral code, and urges her to persuade Gerald not to go with Illingworth. Alone with Gerald, Mrs Arbuthnot tells him her story as if it happened to someone else. Gerald is censorious, saying that a 'nice girl' would not have fallen (Act III, p. 86). Wretchedly, she agrees to let him go; but then Hester bursts in, terrified: Lord Illingworth has tried to kiss her. Gerald threatens him, and Mrs Arbuthnot restrains her son by telling him that Illingworth is his father.

The following day (Act IV), Mrs Allonby and Lady Hunstanton call on Mrs Arbuthnot, but she pleads a headache. When they leave,

CHECK THE BOOK
The three-volume Folio Society edition of Wilde's works published in 1993 contains a moving account of the work of Merlin's father, Vyvyan Holland, in publishing Wilde's collected letters, and includes some of these.

www. CHECK THE NET
The official website of Oscar Wilde offers useful background material – including photographs of the period – to Wilde's life and works. Go to **www.cmgww.com /historic/wilde**

Gerald tells his mother he will demand that Illingworth marry her. She, however, passionately refuses to marry him. Hester arrives and rushes to her support, telling her she wishes to marry Gerald and inviting Mrs Arbuthnot to live abroad with them. The young people go into the garden.

Lord Illingworth arrives; anxious to keep his son, he makes a patronising offer of marriage. Mrs Arbuthnot rejects him, saying that Gerald is now financially independent, thanks to Hester. Illingworth remarks that in polite society it is surprising to meet 'one's mistress, and one's [bastard]' – she strikes him with his own glove before he can utter the offending word (Act IV, p. 111). When he has gone, the young couple return. Gerald sees the glove and asks who has called. His mother replies: 'No one in particular. A man of no importance' (Act IV, p. 112).

Detailed summaries

Act I

Pages 5–10

- Lady Caroline interrogates Hester.
- Gerald tells Lady Hunstanton and the other women his news.

The curtain rises on a formal garden, where Lady Hunstanton's house guests are relaxing. Lady Caroline Pontefract is dividing her time between bullying her husband, Sir John; interrogating Hester Worsley, a young American heiress; and criticising the 'mix' of guests invited by their hostess. Hester is ill at ease with some of the people she has met at the house, notably the cynical Mrs Allonby. Although she too disapproves of Mrs Allonby, Lady Caroline sharply chides Hester as an interfering foreigner who does not appreciate that Mrs Allonby is 'well born' (p. 7). Both Hester and Lady Caroline agree on the charms of another guest, Gerald Arbuthnot, a young bank clerk; nonetheless, Lady Caroline

GLOSSARY

5 *Hunstanton* a small town in Norfolk, where Wilde began the play. It was his habit to name characters after the place where he was writing

6 **muffler** a long woollen scarf, not very suitable for the summer setting of the play

reproves Hester for expressing her interest in a man so directly. Moments later, Lady Hunstanton enters and Lady Caroline smoothly congratulates her on her ability to create an interesting mixture of guests.

Gerald enters, full of excitement. He has been offered a job as secretary to Lady Hunstanton's most distinguished guest, Lord Illingworth – and he hints, discreetly, that his improved salary will put him in a position to court Hester. It is a great opportunity, as Lord Illingworth is talked of as a possible ambassador. Lady Hunstanton dispatches a note to Gerald's mother, telling her the news and inviting her to come to the house that evening to meet Lord Illingworth. Gerald and Hester go for a stroll together.

COMMENTARY

As the curtain rises, the realistic garden setting, shows that the play is **naturalistic** – that is, it will not use poetic language, fantastic locations or bizarre situations but instead appears to imitate real life. The idle chatter makes it clear that the play is to be a social **comedy**. The formal garden also connotes luxurious idleness; the characters are at ease in their chairs and the conversation is apparently aimless.

However, some key conflicts of the play are already at work in the apparently tranquil atmosphere. There is a marked clash between English and American values. Lady Caroline's query: 'Have you any country? What we should call country?', and Hester's answer: 'We have the largest country in the world' (p. 6), reflect very different understandings of the word: Lady Caroline's indicates aristocratic possessiveness and an assumed right to define the worth of a place; Hester's suggests space, liberty and freedom to develop the land as its people wish. There is also conflict between youth and age: Lady Caroline's brisk retort, 'Ah! you must find it very draughty' (p. 6), makes the audience laugh, but also brings the subject to a close, leaving Hester at a loss. Hester's directness sharply contrasts with the hypocrisy of Lady Caroline's rapid switch from criticising Lady Hunstanton – 'Jane mixes too much' (p. 6) – to congratulating her on her 'wonderful power of selection' (p. 8). While this gives Lady Hunstanton a splendid comic entrance, the moment also suggests that the English upper class does not

---

CHECK THE BOOK

Realism and Naturalism, the first volume of J. L. Styan's three-volume *Modern Drama in Theory and Practice* (1981), has a detailed discussion of the complex relationships between different kinds of English and European naturalistic drama across a hundred years. It is worth noting that the plays of Wilde are mentioned not only in this volume but also in the others, which deal with the non-naturalistic modes surrealism and expressionism.

CONTEXT

Most of Oscar Wilde's British contemporaries wrote in a broadly naturalistic style, although they were more timid in their choice of subject matter than many of their European counterparts.

CONTEXT

Henry James' *The American* (1877) contains a speech that perhaps sums up the way Hester is perceived by Lady Caroline. An aristocratic lady says to the rich young American hoping to marry into her family: 'you have been, I frankly confess, less – less peculiar than I expected. It is not your disposition we object to, it is your antecedents. We really cannot reconcile ourselves to a commercial person' (Chapter 18).

GLOSSARY

16   **dry goods** groceries

19   **magic lantern** slide show, cheap entertainment

22   **helpmeet** helpful companion; an archaic term by the 1890s. Used of Eve in the Bible and of the ideal wife in the Book of Common Prayer; suggests a degree of equality

value frankness. The theme of American innocence versus European sophistication was a favourite of the novelist Henry James, Wilde's contemporary, and would have been familiar to many of the original audience. While Hester is clearly a New Woman (see **Historical background: The New Woman** for a discussion of this term), wealthy, independent and able to make her own judgements, including those concerning relationships, her isolation makes her the most vulnerable figure on the stage in this scene.

The differing opinions about the house party – Lady Caroline's private aversion to the mix and Lady Hunstanton's more optimistic view that 'we all do fit in very nicely together' (p. 8) – create **suspense**. How volatile will this combination of characters prove? House parties were popular with the wealthy in late Victorian England; the Prince of Wales (later Edward VII), who admired the play, attended many; they afforded opportunities to exert political or social influence and form relationships. Here Wilde demonstrates that they also involve hard work for the less wealthy: Francis the footman, kept busy fetching cushions and shawls, is the most active figure on stage. Gerald's excited entrance demonstrates the power of this party to change lives. A penniless young man with a chance to prove himself is a very suitable candidate for romantic hero. However, he also seems surprisingly passive, still living with his mother. His entrance is typical: Gerald is always bursting with enthusiasm about the last person to speak to him.

PAGES 10–24

- The guests debate sexual propriety.
- Lord Illingworth displays his wit.
- Lady Stutfield attempts to find a lover.
- Mr Kelvil voices his views on domestic life, and Lord Alfred speaks of money.

Lady Caroline imperiously sends her husband to go and put on his overshoes – perhaps because she has caught sight of two flirtatious women about to enter the garden, Lady Stutfield and Mrs Allonby. The ladies gossip about local sexual scandals and the different standards expected of men and women. Sir John returns with another guest, the MP Mr Kelvil. Lady Caroline at once ensures that her husband sits next to her, leaving Lady Stutfield to flirt with Kelvil, who tells her that he has been writing on the subject of 'Purity' (p. 13), 'the one subject of really national importance, nowadays' (p. 14).

The conversation turns to the role of women in public life; Lord Illingworth enters just as his hostess is announcing that he does not 'value the moral qualities in women as much as he should' (p. 14); and Lady Stutfield goes a little further to describe him excitedly as 'very, very wicked' (p. 14). He wittily expounds his views on a number of subjects – America, universal suffrage, poverty, the aristocracy. It shocks some of the company, and leads Mr Kelvil to question Lord Illingworth's sincerity. Illingworth replies that he is 'Quite serious', but follows this by saying that 'The intellect is not a serious thing' (p. 20). Illingworth and Mrs Allonby rise and leave to inspect a rare orchid in the conservatory.

The guests turn their attention to criticising the two who have just left. As a new guest, Lord Alfred Rufford arrives, the women denigrate Mrs Allonby, implying that she has had several affairs; although there is no evidence, Lady Caroline considers that it is safest to believe the worst of everyone. Mr Kelvil disparages Lord Illingworth's lack of reverence for home life. Lady Stutfield listens to the MP's views on domesticity and the rights of women with apparent fascination until she hears that he has a wife and eight children, whereupon she promptly shifts her attention to Lord Alfred, who tells her with evident pride that he is deeply in debt.

A footman brings a letter from Mrs Arbuthnot, declining the invitation to dine; Lady Hunstanton is disappointed, but 'very pleased' that she will visit that evening, expressing great admiration for Mrs Arbuthnot as a good woman and a pillar of the local church (p. 24). The guests go in to tea, Lady Caroline carefully ensuring that Sir John is too busy carrying her workbasket to walk in with Lady Stutfield.

CONTEXT

In 1890 the shipbuilder Sir Arthur Wilson hosted a party at Tranby Croft. Guests included the Prince of Wales and his current mistress, Lady Daisy Brook. The company played baccarat – a card game illegal in England – and one guest, Sir William Gordon-Cumming, was caught cheating. When this information was leaked, Gordon-Cumming tried to sue, and the Prince of Wales was called as a witness. Gordon-Cumming lost his lawsuit and was obliged to retire from society.

 QUESTION

Examine the different views about the aristocracy presented in the play. Do you agree that the aristocratic characters we see are 'a civilised body' as Lord Illingworth claims (p. 20)?

? QUESTION

Discuss Wilde's use of costumes, **props** and sets in the play. How do particular items such as gloves, shawls and pictures contribute to our experience of the drama, and what sort of decisions might a director need to make about them to get a desired effect?

CONTEXT

Gout is a painful inflammation of the big toe joint, caused by raised levels of uric acid in the blood. In the past it was often associated with the over-indulgent lifestyles of the upper classes.

COMMENTARY

When the young people have left, the atmosphere changes, with their elders free to speak without contradiction about the codes which shape their class. Lady Hunstanton is genuinely pleased at the success of her *'protégé'* Gerald (p. 10). However, as the conversation turns to Lady Pagden's attempts to get rid of a governess 'far too good-looking to be in any respectable household' (p. 11), the audience may wonder if Lady Hunstanton can be trusted in her dealings with people she considers socially beneath her.

In this section the hypocrisy shown by Lady Caroline is revealed as a social rule. The guests ponder the conduct of relationships; nevertheless, this is not a conversation about morality. Mrs Allonby's remark that the country could make her 'unsophisticated' (p. 11) might suggest the traditional conflict between city vice and rural virtue, but Lady Hunstanton at once contradicts this. Local scandal is a source of entertainment, not something to deplore; she cannot even remember whether Lord Belton's death after his wife eloped was caused by 'joy, or gout' (p. 12). Lady Caroline and Mrs Allonby sum up the sexual code of their world when they discuss 'playing with fire' (p. 12). Lady Caroline sees this as endemic among young women; it is clear that she considers it dangerous – but not, evidently, for both sexes. Mrs Allonby views it as a skill to be learned: 'It is the people who don't know how to play with it who get burned up' (p. 12). Nobody seriously objects to the fact that women suffer from being 'burned up' far more than men. Everyone is willing to connive at sexual misdemeanours as long as they have no visible consequences; if, however, there are visible consequences – an illegitimate child, for instance – there will be no mercy.

In a **naturalistic** drama characters do not always state their feelings and intentions. Instead the playwright uses **subtext**: the audience is given clues to unspoken emotions or ideas. Beneath the surface politeness, there are some powerful undercurrents of feeling. Lady Caroline is in a permanent state of jealous anxiety. As Sir John enters with Mr Kelvil she barks commands about overshoes and a sheltered seat. It is comically apparent to the audience that she wants to keep him away from Lady Stutfield – whose gushing interest in Mr Kelvil's favourite subject, 'Purity', reflects her equally unspoken determination to have an affair at this party. She sees no contradiction in her choice of temporary love object. This makes her a figure of fun, but it is clear that Mr Kelvil is as hypocritical as the other guests – he sees his 'Purity' mission as something for 'the poorer classes' (p. 14).

Anticipation has been building about Lord Illingworth from the beginning, and as he walks in to catch Lady Stutfield talking about his wickedness (p. 14), the actor has the opportunity of an entrance demonstrating both wit and authority. His clothes and manner show that he is a **dandy**: in other words, he is as interested in the way a thought is expressed as in its sincerity. In this he is the opposite of Hester. The audience can expect their clash to be another important strand in the play. It is clear, though, that this will not be treated simplistically. The stage picture is striking, with the dandified lord at the centre of a circle of admirers feeding him lines to which he can make clever replies. However, he is the most radical political thinker on the stage. Illingworth's diagnosis of East End unrest is sharp: 'It is the problem of slavery. And we are trying to solve it by amusing the slaves' (p. 18). For the first time in the play, members of the upper class consider the world beyond their own circle. Curiously, the only character who might share Lord Illingworth's sentiments is Hester. As he leaves with Mrs Allonby, the remaining guests confirm their lack of concern for the wider world. Lady Stutfield's flirtations reveal both Kelvil's hypocrisy and Lord Alfred's contempt for his creditors. Serious political thought has vanished with the apparently frivolous Illingworth.

While this section has no significant action, the seemingly idle chatter has laid the groundwork for the whole play. The audience is now well aware that any visible evidence of sexual misdemeanours on the part of a female character will have painful consequences.

CONTEXT

Lord Illingworth is not exaggerating when he talks of 'amusing the slaves' (p. 18). Charles Booth's multi-volumed report on the London poor appeared piecemeal between 1887 and 1903 and shocked most of those who read it. The report made it clear that almost a third of the city's population lived in poverty, and that the wages of working people were too low to help them out of it.

CONTEXT

Wilde said that Act I of *A Woman of No Importance* was written to answer accusations that his earlier play, *Lady Windermere's Fan*, lacked action. In an interview with Gilbert Burgess of the *Sketch* before the first night of *An Ideal Husband* Wilde said: 'There was absolutely no action at all. It was a perfect act.'

GLOSSARY

28   **made love to**
make amorous
conversation or woo,
pay court

29   **laurels** trophies

31   **The Book of Life**
Bible

**CHECK
THE BOOK**

Pierre Choderlos de
Laclos' novel *Les
Liaisons dangereuses*
(1782) relates in the
form of letters the
seduction of an
innocent young
woman for a wager
between two
corrupt aristocrats.
Wilde, and many of
his audience, would
have known the
novel, although
the plot as it stood
could not possibly
have been shown
on the stage of the
1890s.

**CHECK
THE FILM**

*Les Liaisons
dangereuses* has
been filmed several
times, most famously
by Stephen Frears in
1988, while Roger
Kumble's *Cruel
Intentions* (1999)
transfers this plot to
an American high
school.

PAGES 24–32

- Lord Illingworth and Mrs Allonby laugh about the other guests.
- They meet Hester and Gerald.
- Mrs Allonby issues a challenge to Lord Illingworth.
- We hear about the woman of no importance.

Mrs Allonby and Lord Illingworth re-enter and comment in their turn upon the other guests. Mrs Allonby acidly notes Lady Caroline's jealousy over Sir John, and they both express amusement at Lady Stutfield's attempts to flirt with everyone, including Lord Illingworth himself. The young couple return, and Mrs Allonby and Lord Illingworth hold brief separate conversations with them. When they have left, it is clear Lord Illingworth has been charmed by Gerald, but Mrs Allonby finds Hester's forthrightness irritating. Both of them disparage the 'Puritan' tendency they detect in her, but Lord Illingworth adds that she is attractive. Mrs Allonby then challenges Lord Illingworth to kiss Hester; they speculate whether Hester will react to this with anger or desire.

Having arranged their wager, they continue to flirt with each other. Mrs Allonby makes a veiled promise that things may go further if Lord Illingworth succeeds in kissing Hester. Tea is announced, but they decide to stay in the garden, where Lord Illingworth notices Mrs Arbuthnot's letter lying on the table. The handwriting seems familiar; it reminds him of someone he knew: 'A woman of no importance' (p. 32). The curtain falls on this clear hint that there is some kind of history between Lord Illingworth and Mrs Arbuthnot.

COMMENTARY

Lord Illingworth's intelligence is matched by Mrs Allonby's. Their mutual attraction has already revealed itself **subtextually**. Although they have exchanged few words, earlier both of them sprang to their feet at exactly the same moment (p. 20), as if to indicate that their thoughts about the conversation (and desire to escape it) were identical. When they are alone together after their meeting with Gerald and Hester, they speak in short sentences that contrast sharply with the leisurely speech of the others. Lord Illingworth's use of the fencing **metaphor** (p. 31) suits their energy and playfulness. The connotations of swordplay also suggest danger. What seems to be a budding romance between them gradually takes on a more sinister colouring. Mrs Allonby's resentment of eighteen-year-old Hester's beauty is a surprise (p. 27): this perceptive woman is behaving like Lady Caroline. The plot to kiss Hester seems at first sight relatively innocuous; however, it suggests that Lord Illingworth may habitually use his sexual charm as a means to get what he wants.

'The Book of Life', Lord Illingworth says to Mrs Allonby, 'begins with a man and a woman in a garden' (p. 31). It is a flirtatious remark; the setting suggests that they might play at Adam and Eve in the Garden of Eden – but the bet may indicate that he also sees himself as the serpent threatening Hester's innocence. Mrs Allonby's retort – 'It ends with Revelations' – maintains the flirtation. But it is also a joke about theatre. It reminds the audience they are watching a **well-made play** which follows the conventional Victorian pattern, with a plot hinging on 'revelations' – generally about past sexual or political indiscretions that could ruin someone's present happiness. Bang on cue, Lord Illingworth spots Mrs Arbuthnot's letter, a common device for imparting such revelations.

The curtain comes down on a note of **suspense**. It is plain that Gerald's mother is a major character, the **eponymous** 'woman of no importance' (p. 32), but the audience has no clue about the sort of person she will turn out to be. In the hypocritical world Wilde has shown, the pillar of the church so admired by Lady Hunstanton could turn out to be a blackmailer, Illingworth's former mistress or even his abandoned wife – all of these would be strong possibilities on the London stage of the 1890s. The only certainty is that the meeting between Mrs Arbuthnot and Lord Illingworth will be theatrically exciting, and the audience can spend the interval in pleasurable speculation.

? QUESTION

Part of the skill of a writer of well-made plays was to provide an exciting curtain at the end of each act. Examine the curtain lines in the play and discuss their effectiveness. What aspects of the action might the audience enjoy debating during the intervals?

ACT II

PAGES 32–41

- The women relax after dinner without the men.
- Mrs Allonby speaks of life with her husband, Ernest.
- They consider the Ideal Man.

The women are served with after-dinner coffee in the drawing-room. They feel able to relax while the men are having their port, and the conversation turns to the important topic of how to keep them under control. Mrs Allonby complains of her own marriage: she finds it stale, although she cannot accuse her husband, Ernest, of anything worse than being calm, faithful and totally uninteresting. They conclude that the middle classes have happier marriages than the gentry, but are not certain why. Lady Caroline suggests the problem lies with the frivolity of upper-class women; Mrs Allonby locates it in the dreary common sense of their menfolk. The conversation shifts to the topic of the 'Ideal Man'. Mrs Allonby offers a scandalous but witty outline of his character: he should always keep his relationship with a woman volatile and **paradoxical** – 'talk to us as if we were goddesses, and treat us as if we were children' (p. 39). But there are, she maintains, 'just four in London' (p. 41) – though who they are is never revealed …

COMMENTARY

The opening of Act II provides an amusing contrast to that of Act I. Although in both cases the curtain rises on members of the upper classes at leisure, the tone is completely different. In the presence of men – even the compliant Sir John – the conversation was formal; here women talk with remarkable frankness. It is interesting that although each one has a different view of the struggle between the sexes, everybody assumes without question that there *is* a struggle.

Mrs Allonby sees relationships in terms of ownership, with men 'always trying to escape from us'; Lady Stutfield seems stuck in the helpless dependency she uses as a flirtation device: 'Men are so very,

very heartless'; Lady Caroline sees marriage as a necessary tool to control men and keep them 'in their proper place' (p. 33). Mrs Allonby makes the most apparently radical statement of all with her assertion that 'we don't belong to any one' (p. 34) – but it proves merely a figure of speech through which she claims the freedom to make her own sexual choices.

Not one of the group has any interest in social change. Nevertheless, the fourth Married Women's Property Bill was currently being debated (see the discussion in **Historical background: The Angel in the House**), and Mrs Allonby's topical allusion acts as a reminder that these women inhabit a changing world. Lady Caroline's rigid views may spring from the enforced dependency of married life experienced by her generation. Rich Englishwomen would soon have some, at least, of the economic power (and liberty) that Hester already possesses.

There is a contradiction at the heart of this scene. The after-dinner ritual of sexual separation – designed to permit men to consume port, cigars and risqué stories – would have been familiar to the better-off members of Wilde's audience. While on the one hand it seems to create an interval of intimacy and privacy, it is also part of an elaborate code of manners with its own conventions. It is notable, for instance, that none of the women seem to feel inhibited by the silent servants busily serving coffee – even though Mrs Allonby here challenges the boundaries of what may be discussed in polite society. Indeed, Wilde himself is challenging the censor; the **subtext** here is charged with Mrs Allonby's sexual boredom. As she dwells at length on the size and shape of Ernest's chin, the word takes on an almost surreal tone, suggesting the ladies are talking in code about male sexual inadequacy. When Mrs Allonby lists the qualities of the Ideal Man, she is following an old stage tradition in the **comedy of manners**; the heroine often spelled out to the hero how she would expect him to behave after marriage in what was known as a **proviso scene**. Here, however, Mrs Allonby's demands are appropriate to a lover, not a husband, and she states outright of marriage that 'The institution is wrong' (p. 39). Yet her preference for manipulating men, rather than for the blatant affairs that Lady Stutfield is constantly courting, implies that she will not risk her status by getting 'burned'.

CONTEXT

Wilde's next play was to have the title *An Ideal Husband*. In it the woman who thinks that she is married to the 'ideal of my life' (Act II, *Complete Works*, p. 552) has to come to terms with the fact that he has sold state secrets for money; he complains that women place men on a pedestal when they should forgive their weaknesses. The nearest thing to an 'ideal husband' in the play is the witty Lord Goring, whose fiancée says that she wants no such thing, and would prefer her husband to 'be what he chooses' (Act IV, p. 582).

GLOSSARY

44   **iron Exhibition**
the World's Fair in
Chicago in 1893 was
an internationally
famous event and was
held in a large and
specially constructed
building of glass and
iron. Lady Hunstanton
may be typically dizzy
in her failure to
recollect its name
correctly, or she may
be deliberately
disparaging a source
of American pride

44   **leper in purple**
leprosy, a disfiguring
skin disease, was once
considered to be
extremely contagious,
and lepers were
shunned. Purple is the
colour associated with
royalty and the
aristocracy; members
of the House of Lords
wore purple cloaks
trimmed with ermine

CONTEXT

A dowager is a
widow whose title
derives from her
late husband. Here
Mrs Allonby uses
the term in a more
colloquial (and
rude) sense to
mean old women
generally, as Lady
Caroline's husband
is still alive.

PAGES 42–51

- Hester preaches against sexual sinners.
- We meet Mrs Arbuthnot.
- We hear a little of Lord Illingworth's past.

Lady Hunstanton draws attention to Hester sitting quietly listening to the conversation. Hester expresses extreme disapproval of everything she has heard and contrasts it with the directness and democracy of America. In a long tirade she calls England 'a leper in purple ... a dead thing smeared with gold' (p. 44). She has particular scorn for Lord Henry Weston, a corrupt aristocrat who has caused the 'ruin' of many women – although she says that these women too should suffer: 'Let all women who have sinned be punished' (p. 45).

Mrs Arbuthnot slips quietly into the drawing-room, starting as she hears Hester proclaim this. She is also disconcerted to find such a large gathering. Hester's lofty moral tone is undermined by Lady Hunstanton, who remarks: 'you looked very pretty while you said it, which is much more important' (p. 47). She puts Hester at a further disadvantage by pointing out that Lord Henry is Lady Caroline's brother. Abashed, Hester hastens to apologise. Lady Stutfield and Mrs Allonby decide to slip away, 'to get away from the dowagers and the dowdies' (p. 48). The conversation among the women remaining turns to the offer that Lord Illingworth has made to Gerald. Mrs Arbuthnot says that she has never met Lord Illingworth, and Lady Hunstanton gives her a short sketch of his pedigree, explaining how as a younger son he inherited his title unexpectedly. Upon hearing this, Mrs Arbuthnot expresses an urgent need to see Gerald at once.

COMMENTARY

The issue of manners continues to be important in this section. Lady Hunstanton is forced to work hard here as hostess of this combustible social mix. She is guiltily aware that Hester may have been upset by the conversation. Mrs Allonby's cool remark, 'that will do her so much good!' (p. 42), is interesting – has she noticed Hester and deliberately tried to shock her? Much will depend on where the director chooses to place Hester: well hidden, as if embarrassed by what she hears, she will seem more vulnerable; if she is in clear sight, she will look more like a spy. While Lady Hunstanton struggles to defuse the situation by explaining that she need not 'believe' all the opinions expressed, Hester makes things worse, effectively calling the women liars (p. 42). Offered a cue to improve her manners as Lady Hunstanton slips into politely formal enquiries about America, Hester refuses it. Spontaneously and without the need for speech, the circle decides to use its code of politeness to punish her. Lady Caroline, ostensibly offering comfort for the gaffe about her brother, stresses the impropriety of Hester's outburst, describing it as a 'little speech, if I may so term it' (p. 47). After this, nobody speaks to her.

However, Hester's isolation gives her an opportunity to observe Mrs Arbuthnot at close quarters. The quiet entry of this important character, mysterious in her veil, has been in its way as dramatic as the more extrovert first appearance of Lord Illingworth. There is a ghostly quality to the drapery over her head and her choice to appear without being announced that will make the audience pay close attention to her as she responds to the story of Illingworth's family.

PAGES 52–7

- We meet Dr Daubeny, the Archdeacon.
- Mrs Arbuthnot makes difficulties about Gerald's new job.
- Gerald asks Lord Illingworth to deal with his mother.

The men return to the drawing-room. We meet a new character, Dr Daubeny, the Archdeacon, and Lady Hunstanton laments the absence of his wife. 'Headache as usual, I suppose?' she asks (p. 52). Lord Illingworth goes directly to the two flirts, Mrs Allonby and Lady Stutfield, and their conversation continues on the previous

---

CONTEXT

The line about English society lying 'like a leper in purple. It sits like a dead thing smeared with gold' (p. 44) was cut after the first night in London, when it was loudly booed. However, Wilde kept it in the published edition, and on the play's first night in New York it drew prolonged applause.

CONTEXT

Mrs Arbuthnot's sudden arrival prompts Lady Hunstanton to ring the bell to summon the footman to come and take Mrs Arbuthnot's things (p. 46). Mrs Arbuthnot has been socially awkward in not arriving by the front door, where her wrap would be taken and she would be properly announced to the company

GLOSSARY

55 **duffer** schoolboy slang for a dunce

theme: the annoying puritanism of Hester. Lord Illingworth claims he can 'convert' her in less than a week (p. 53).

Gerald enters, concerned for his mother, who says that she is unwell and wants to go home. Despite this, he insists that she should meet Lord Illingworth. When they are introduced, Illingworth is plainly shocked. Mrs Arbuthnot speaks in a cold, reserved manner: 'There can be nothing in common between you and my son, Lord Illingworth' (p. 55). While her argument seems to be that Gerald is unqualified for the post, it is clear that her unwillingness is rooted in hostility to her son's potential employer. Mrs Allonby summons Lord Illingworth, apparently piqued at his interest in another woman.

As the party begins to shift to the music-room and Lady Hunstanton smoothly announces that 'Miss Worsley is going to play' (p. 56), Gerald, impervious to the atmosphere, rushes to ask Lord Illingworth to convince his mother that his offer is serious. Illingworth agrees, and when Lady Hunstanton remarks that 'she will have a great deal to thank you for' (p. 57), it becomes impossible for Mrs Arbuthnot to avoid the interview.

COMMENTARY

As the men return, the atmosphere changes. With the arrival of Dr Daubeny, the Archdeacon, we might expect some pious platitudes to unite the party. In fact, his first mention of his wife – 'a perfect martyr. But she is happiest alone' (p. 52) – develops the idea that the sexes behave differently when apart. Watched by the silent Hester, Mrs Arbuthnot also remains silent. She in turn spends some time watching Lord Illingworth as he enters without seeing her. This intense triangle of observation will ensure that the audience is attentive to the facial expressions and **body language** of the three characters; they will not miss what is perhaps the real beginning of Hester's education about sexual saints and sinners.

There is a shift here in the relationship between Lord Illingworth and Mrs Allonby. We know he lies when assuring her that while with the men he was too bored to speak, as the Archdeacon has just praised his 'most entertaining' conversation (p. 52). As they return to the topic of Hester, he speaks of an intent to 'convert' (p. 53) rather than to kiss her. This suggests, perhaps, that his intention is to seduce her. The stakes seem suddenly higher and the isolated girl more vulnerable. As Illingworth goes to meet Mrs Arbuthnot, he and Mrs Allonby seem on the verge of a quarrel. Previously they took a mutual pleasure in wit, now she finishes his **epigram** 'All women become like their mothers. That is their tragedy' with 'No man does. That is his.' The little competition makes him sarcastic: 'What a delightful mood you are in tonight!' (p. 54).

The poised Lord Illingworth is thus already at a disadvantage when he is disconcerted by the sight of Mrs Arbuthnot. His reaction may be enough for the more perceptive in the audience to deduce the true state of affairs. Even those who do not will notice that the sweet and simple woman described by Lady Hunstanton is remarkably rude: 'Lord Illingworth is very good, I am sure, to interest himself in you *for the moment*' (p. 54, my italics). Mrs Allonby's jealousy of 'the lady in black velvet' (p. 56) and Illingworth's exploitation of it makes the figure of the saintly Mrs Arbuthnot even more interesting to the audience as the atmosphere vibrates with sexual tension.

The Archdeacon provides an absurd counterpoint to this theme. The more we hear about his unseen wife and her ailments, the more hilariously exaggerated her image in our mind becomes. However, it also raises some questions about the way this couple treat each other. Does she use her illness as an opportunity to get rid of him? 'Her deafness is a great privation to her. She can't even hear my sermons now' (p. 56). Or does it give him an excuse to socialise alone? One of the couple appears to be exercising power over the other – but which? The comic interlude sustains the theme of a power struggle between the sexes; the power struggle between women is also evident as Lady Hunstanton ensures that with a violin wedged under her chin, Hester can make no more provocative remarks. All these tensions increase the audience's anticipation of the confrontation between Illingworth and the 'woman of no importance'.

CONTEXT

Among the well-to-do there was an elaborate dress code for the bereaved. Mrs Arbuthnot's black dress may indicate that she is passing as a recent widow, or she may have chosen it as part of her self-effacing lifestyle. Velvet, however, is a luxurious material designed to make the skin glow, and it clearly suits her well enough to arouse suspicion in Mrs Allonby. Mrs Arbuthnot may have a streak of personal vanity.

PAGES 57–64

- We learn that Lord Illingworth is Gerald's father.
- Lord Illingworth and Mrs Arbuthnot argue.
- Lord Illingworth says Gerald will not forgive his mother if he discovers the truth about his parentage.
- Gerald is summoned, and Mrs Arbuthnot gives in.

GLOSSARY

58 **twenty-one**
at that time, the age when a person could marry without parental consent. Lord Illingworth was thus legally free to marry Rachel

Throughout the action hints have been dropped; the mystery is now revealed with Lord Illingworth's opening remark: 'So that is our son, Rachel!' (p. 57). The conversation reveals their past history: when Illingworth was twenty-one, they began an affair; when Rachel became pregnant, he refused to marry her. His mother offered her money, while his father tried to insist on marriage. Rachel left to bring up Gerald alone.

CHECK THE BOOK

Peter Raby's *Oscar Wilde* (1988) usefully analyses *A Woman of No Importance* in terms of the conflict between the aristocracy and the middle classes.

Illingworth is determined to play a part in his son's life, and that Gerald will prosper through his influence, instead of being an 'underpaid clerk in a small provincial bank' (p. 60). When Mrs Arbuthnot refuses to allow this he resorts to blackmail, pointing out that the moral code in which she has raised Gerald will turn him against her if he discovers his illegitimacy. She responds with an appeal to Illingworth's mercy. Gerald enters at this crucial moment, and Illingworth challenges her directly by asking if she has reasons she would prefer to divulge privately. Defeated, she replies that she has not, and the matter is settled. The curtain falls on Illingworth's triumph.

COMMENTARY

Although the subject matter of this scene was a staple of the Victorian theatre, the complexity of the characters and the number of conflicts embodied in it give it great energy and power. Wilde develops the tensions between public manners and private spaces established at the beginning of this act. Illingworth's use of Mrs Arbuthnot's Christian name establishes a new tone of quiet informality. The balance of sympathy constantly shifts. Mrs

Arbuthnot's reproaches are just, but her tone is self-indulgent as she refers to 'the child who, as far as you are concerned, might have died of hunger and of want' (p. 58). Illingworth deflates this piece of **melodrama** with the retort: 'My mother offered you six hundred a year' (p. 59). On the other hand, Wilde's audience would have been in no doubt about the meaning of that six hundred pounds. It is effectively a payment for services rendered from a class which sees marriage solely as a means of preserving or advancing itself, and relationships with the lower orders as mere diversions; to accept would have made Rachel, in her own eyes at least, a prostitute. Mrs Arbuthnot has clearly and correctly read this money as a pay-off to an unwanted encumbrance.

Alongside these conflicts is another, presented with sly **irony** – a parental row. Illingworth may have a logical point to make when he talks about Gerald's right to a career, but his peevish generalisation – 'What a typical woman you are!' (p. 60) – is a comical contrast to the elegant **epigrams** about women he used in the first act; as the butt of Wilde's humour he seems more human. Mrs Arbuthnot, too, takes on a more familiar and gentle tone when she abandons her formal coldness for a passionate speech and calls Illingworth 'George'. The interchange reveals new facets to both characters, and underlines their mutual vulnerability. With the entry of Gerald, their behaviour changes for the worse. If Illingworth blackmails Mrs Arbuthnot by threatening to reveal the truth, then Mrs Arbuthnot uses moral blackmail to make Gerald feel guilty: 'I didn't know you were so anxious to leave me' (p. 63). As the curtain falls it seems clear that despite Illingworth's victory, nothing is really 'settled'.

See **Text 1** of **Extended commentaries** for further discussion of part of this section.

CONTEXT

The amount mentioned by Mrs Arbuthnot, six hundred pounds a year, was more or less what Wilde earned when he edited the *Woman's World*, and enabled him to keep a stylishly decorated house in Tite Street. We should understand it as being enough to keep a family in some style.

ACT III

PAGES 64–71

- Lord Illingworth tries to turn Gerald against his mother.
- He tells Gerald how to be a dandy.
- Illingworth explains women and the nature of love to Gerald.

After the stresses of the previous act, the curtain rises on a quiet personal conversation between men as Gerald and Lord Illingworth sit and talk in the picture gallery. Illingworth probes discreetly to find out how much Gerald knows about his birth. Gerald innocently says that he thinks his mother 'must have married beneath her' (p. 66). Illingworth subtly undermines the role of mothers: 'good women have such limited views of life, their horizon is so small, their interests are so petty, aren't they?' (p. 66).

He deftly moves on to the subject of modernity. He begins by pronouncing that 'The future belongs to the dandy', that success is grounded in the ability to 'dominate a London dinner-table' (p. 67), and goes on to explain to a puzzled Gerald how to do this by attaining the goodwill of women. He assumes women lack logic but have power through dependency: 'The tyranny of the weak over the strong' (p. 69). He has no time for marriage and assumes (ironically in the presence of his lower-middle-class illegitimate son) that passion is the privilege of the upper classes; this allows him to boast of his own aristocratic lineage – just as we glimpse Mrs Arbuthnot outside the window.

COMMENTARY

This scene is set against a background of painted images, reflecting the calculated artifice of Lord Illingworth's behaviour. This is the first scene in the play without women and he takes advantage of the chance to speak freely about the opposite sex just as the ladies do in Act II. At some point he gives Gerald a cigarette (later Illingworth informs Lady Hunstanton that he has been 'giving [Gerald] the best of advice … and the best of cigarettes' p. 71). This reinforces the image of a private male space, the 'smoking-room' where Victorian men traditionally told racy anecdotes. Plainly, Illingworth is setting out to consolidate his position. His **body language** initially puts Gerald at a disadvantage. Illingworth is *'lolling on a sofa'* while Gerald is *'in a chair'* like a candidate at a job interview – and perhaps this is how he interprets this encounter (p. 64).

For once, Wilde makes Illingworth the butt of the joke with Gerald's remark about his father. He recovers from the unwitting slight rapidly, and the fact that he immediately rises and *'puts his hand on* GERALD*'s shoulder'* (p. 66) suggests that he wants to put the young man more at ease. His language is caressing, dwelling on Gerald's name throughout as he dwelt on Rachel's in Act II. He is careful not to anger Gerald by a direct attack on his mother, but generalises about women in elegantly structured sentences. Ending with a **rhetorical question** – 'aren't they?' (p. 66) – flatters Gerald by assuming that he is a man of experience. Loaded questions such as 'You want to be modern, don't you, Gerald?' are impossible for Gerald to contradict (p. 67).

Gerald, in contrast, speaks like a schoolboy. He uses the word 'awfully' a great deal. He either agrees with Lord Illingworth with his usual bouncing enthusiasm or asks questions based on **clichés** rather than reflection, such as: 'haven't women got a refining influence?' (p. 69). This could have come straight from Mr Kelvil's ramblings on 'Purity'.

It is interesting that while Lord Illingworth initially seems to be simply displaying his dandified persona as in Act I, he now has an agenda – to draw Gerald into his world. Although he has promised Mrs Arbuthnot that he will keep her secret, he seems to be constantly on the edge of revealing it, so the audience is in **suspense** throughout the interview. We wonder if he intends to reveal it in order to make Gerald despise his mother. The 'advice' about women sounds at times like a witty performance: 'Women are pictures. Men are problems' (p. 68). However, Illingworth's bitterness about the 'tyranny of the weak' could be seen as a comment on his last conversation with Mrs Arbuthnot. His diagnosis that 'Every

CONTEXT

Wilde caused outrage by taking a curtain call after the successful first night of his play *Lady Windermere's Fan* with a cigarette in his hand. Smoking in public or in mixed company was frowned upon – although in the original production of *A Woman of No Importance* Lord Illingworth and Mrs Allonby smoked together.

CONTEXT

Illingworth explains to Gerald how to acquire the reputation of having the 'most perfect social tact' at the end of one's 'first season' (p. 68). The social season was the period when the aristocracy and the court scheduled major social events, operating an informal marriage market.

CONTEXT

Burke's Peerage, Baronetage and Knightage, which was first published in 1826, listed all the current peers of the realm. G. E. Cokayne's *Complete Peerage* also detailed their ancestry and was first published in 1884. The **allusion** to 'fiction' may be a hint that some men have inherited titles even though they are not actually the sons of their named father.

GLOSSARY

71 **Dorcas** in the Bible Dorcas is a woman who is 'full of good works' and makes 'coats and garments' (Acts 9:36–9)

73 **Drawing-room** short for withdrawing-room, a place for quiet conversation

77 **maxim** motto or phrase offering guidance for living

woman is a rebel, and usually in wild revolt against herself' (p. 69) can also be interpreted in several ways. It might be advice on how to be a successful seducer. It could suggest he is anticipating his attempt to kiss Hester. It might be a memory of his courtship of Rachel.

The reference to 'the Peerage' being 'the best thing in fiction the English have ever done' (pp. 70–1) is clearly a joke, and while Illingworth's pride in being one of 'us Harfords' (p. 70) is expressed in a rather flippant way, it seems real. This is surprising in the light of his earlier remarks about 'The English country gentleman' (Act I, p. 19). It suggests that however passionate his relationship with a woman 'in wild revolt against herself' (p. 69), the aristocratic lord would never have contemplated marrying Rachel.

PAGES 71–9

- Lady Hunstanton struggles to keep the conversation light.
- The guests discuss morality and the secret of life.
- The party begins to break up.

The company is beginning to reassemble. As she enters with the Archdeacon, Lady Hunstanton tries to bring everyone together in conversation. She invites Mrs Arbuthnot into the room with a polite enquiry about her 'embroidery', but gets only the briefest of replies (p. 71). Lady Hunstanton smoothly glosses over Mrs Arbuthnot's abrupt response by asking the Archdeacon about his wife; Mrs Daubeny, he informs her, 'is very much interested in her own health' (p. 72). She next turns to Lord Illingworth for some lively opinions. When he offers a typical Illingworth **paradox** – 'The only difference between the saint and the sinner is that every saint has a past, and every sinner has a future' (p. 72) – she playfully allies herself with Mrs Arbuthnot as too 'well brought up' to understand him. Mrs Arbuthnot replies that she would be 'sorry to follow Lord Illingworth in any of his opinions', which seems to irritate Gerald (p. 72).

Lady Caroline continues to fret about Sir John. Lady Hunstanton mentions that he is in the 'Yellow Drawing-room' with Lady Stutfield (p. 73), and his wife instantly goes to fetch him, only for him to enter with Mrs Allonby moments later. Lady Stutfield also returns with Mr Kelvil, and Lord Illingworth flirts with both women. As Lord Alfred joins the party the conversation turns to the subject of forgiveness, and Mrs Arbuthnot asserts that women should never forgive 'The ruin of another woman's life' (p. 76). Lady Hunstanton assumes that this is a generality rather than a personal statement and says that there are 'admirable homes' for such women, adding that 'the secret of life is to take things very, very easily' (p. 76). The rest of the company add their opinions of life and Lord Illingworth offers a number of witty remarks while flirting with Lady Hunstanton. The carriage arrives for the Archdeacon, and despite the early hour the party begins to break up. As the guests drift away, Illingworth and Mrs Allonby decide to go and look at the moon, accompanied by Gerald, while Lady Caroline continues her pursuit of Sir John.

COMMENTARY

After the intense and outspoken conversation between the two men, the action and dialogue become much less direct and the **subtext** more complex. Lady Hunstanton – probably unconsciously – sums up the way this exclusive little group goes through the motions of religious observance without much thought: 'I suppose I am too old now to learn. Except from you, dear Archdeacon, when you are in your nice pulpit. But then I always know what you are going to say' (p. 71). Mrs Arbuthnot's very brusque response to the question about her embroidery, 'I am always at work' (p. 71), may reflect her dislike of this genteel hypocrisy as well as her resentment of Illingworth. It is also an implied reproach: to the upper classes in general for their idleness; and to Illingworth, by letting him know how hard her life has been. The embroidery might be a source of income, or simply one of the few activities open to a woman who feels unable to permit herself a rich social life.

The Archdeacon's account of his wife's ailments puts a stop to this line of conversation. It provides the audience with a laugh and Lady Hunstanton with a welcome break from her struggle to coax

CHECK THE BOOK

In Nathaniel Hawthorne's *The Scarlet Letter* (1850) Hester Prynne earns her living by needlework, one of many echoes of Hawthorne's novel in this play. Hester uses her skill to cover the letter A she is forced to wear on her breast as a punishment for adultery in rich embroidery.

CHECK THE BOOK

Nineteenth-century literature was often sentimental about the 'saintly' female invalid – Beth March in Louisa M. Alcott's *Little Women* (1868–9) is perhaps the most familiar example. In contrast, Charlotte Perkins Gilman's 'The Yellow Wallpaper' (1892) is a horrific account of enforced rest which drives an intelligent young woman to a state of near-madness.

Mrs Arbuthnot into her circle. It also gives us an image of loneliness, a very real threat to Mrs Arbuthnot at this time. Lord Illingworth's remark about saints and sinners constitutes an **ambiguous** challenge to her. It can be understood as an appeal for forgiveness and a chance to know his son; but it can also be seen as a threat to reveal her 'past'. The rudeness of her reply suggests that this is how she reads the situation.

Unfortunately, however, Mrs Arbuthnot's ungraciousness serves to develop the bond between Illingworth and Gerald – especially as it is followed by the little comedy centred on Lady Caroline's fussy jealousy. This seems to bear out everything Illingworth has been saying about women's 'tyranny'. It is hard not to wonder whether Lady Hunstanton sends Lady Caroline off to the wrong room on purpose, especially as she is still within earshot for the comment that Lady Stutfield 'is just as sympathetic about one thing as she is about another. A beautiful nature' (p. 73). Similarly, we may suspect her of sharing a joke with Sir John and Mrs Allonby when she mentions that 'Caroline has been looking everywhere' (p. 73). Certainly, nobody bothers to go after her. It is quite clear that at least one of the two flirts has had a dull time. Lady Stutfield is exhausted by the topic of bimetallism, and in both cases the men have clearly done all the talking!

Mrs Arbuthnot makes a very definite withdrawal from the conversation with her remark about forgiveness and 'ruin' – strongly emphasised by her walk to the back of the stage. The stage direction is placed directly after this speech, suggesting that in doing so she is making a silent comment to Illingworth rather than responding uncomfortably to Lady Hunstanton's cheery dismissiveness about 'people of that kind' (p. 76).

At this point there is a slight shift in the tone of the dialogue: with five members of the party sharing the line 'the secret of life is …' the dialogue becomes formal, closer to opera than to drama (p. 76). The contrast in verbal styles gives the exchange a musical quality: Lady Hunstanton softly twittering, Mrs Allonby harder and more concise, Lady Stutfield with her wistful repetitions, Mr Kelvil all pompous masculinity like a big brass tuba, and Illingworth finishing the section by twisting the phrase with a decisive snap. While the characters all have different opinions, the musicality of the exchange implies that at bottom all the group are in harmony. Meanwhile, the silence of Mrs Arbuthnot at the back of the stage – a commanding position for an actress, allowing us to see her reactions to everything – stresses her 'outsider' status. We have seen her isolated on the stage before, but this time her position seems to have been consciously chosen, an act of defiance.

Lord Illingworth's overt flirtation with Mrs Allonby may also be an attempt to get Mrs Arbuthnot's attention. It does not seem to work until Gerald, with a comical lack of sophistication, invites himself to go out with them and view the moon. The rapidity with which Illingworth agrees to break up his romantic twosome is hardly flattering to Mrs Allonby.

PAGES 79–88

- Mrs Arbuthnot learns Hester's views on morality.
- She tells Gerald about Lord Illingworth's past.
- Hester is shocked by Illingworth's attempt to kiss her, and the relationship between Gerald and Illingworth is revealed.

Mrs Arbuthnot stops Gerald and demands they leave; he insists on saying goodbye to Lord Illingworth, and she is left alone and worried. Hester enters, making friendly overtures, confident that unlike the rest Mrs Arbuthnot shares her views. Mrs Arbuthnot agrees with her that 'A woman who has sinned should be punished' – even at the expense of her children (p. 80). Hester urges Mrs Arbuthnot to persuade Gerald not to leave, and goes to fetch him. Lady Caroline enters briefly, hunting Sir John, and Gerald follows.

Mrs Arbuthnot appeals to Gerald to stay; he is angry, accusing her of forcing him to give up his 'one chance in life' (p. 83). He tells her he loves Hester and this chance will allow him to marry her. Mrs Arbuthnot responds bitterly, 'I fear you need have no hopes of Miss

? QUESTION

Lady Hunstanton speaks of 'thunder in the air' (Act IV, p. 89) during the evening. What **subtextual** conflicts can you detect among the characters in Act III?

CONTEXT

Hester's views on the 'sins of the parents' (p. 80) are based on Exodus 20:3–5: 'Thou shalt have no other gods … I the Lord thy God am a jealous God, visiting the iniquity of the fathers upon the children …' This is the first of the Ten Commandments, and it is not concerned with sexual morality, but rather the sin of idolatry. Interestingly too, it is the sin of the *fathers* to be punished. Not for the first time, Hester seems to have got her Bible references confused. There may also be a sly hint that Mrs Arbuthnot's true sin is the one forbidden here – idolatry – in that she has made Gerald the centre of her life for partly selfish reasons.

Worsley. I know her views on life' (p. 83). Only momentarily troubled, Gerald replies that he still has ambition. When his mother is unresponsive he asks her why she objects to Lord Illingworth. She tells him the story of a young woman who had a relationship with Illingworth, but does not reveal that she is that 'lost soul' who once 'trusted in him' and 'loved him' (p. 86). Gerald is unmoved, saying 'the girl was just as much to blame' for living with him unmarried. 'No nice girl would', he announces smugly (p. 86). Defeated, Mrs Arbuthnot withdraws her objection – only for Gerald's pleasure to be interrupted by the entrance of Hester. She is deeply distressed after being 'Horribly insulted' by Lord Illingworth (p. 87). As Illingworth enters, Gerald threatens to kill him. Mrs Arbuthnot drags him back, exclaiming, 'Stop, Gerald, stop! He is your own father!' (p. 88). The curtain remains up for a few minutes, allowing the characters to respond to this information.

COMMENTARY

The struggle over Gerald intensifies with Mrs Arbuthnot's imperious call to prevent him leaving with Illingworth. She has now abandoned the relatively tactful arguments of Act II for direct rudeness. Alone on stage, she says aloud, 'Let him leave me if he chooses, but not with him' (p. 79). This is one of very few **soliloquies** in the play. It was common in **melodrama** for characters to express their emotions to the audience, but the conventions of **naturalism** did not permit such an obviously theatrical device. Here it can be understood as a prayer, showing Mrs Arbuthnot's willingness to sacrifice her son's company and her likeness to the religious Hester.

The exchange between the two women is fraught with **irony**; Mrs Arbuthnot's speeches are notably briefer, suggesting the suppressed emotion behind them. It is clearly important to her to raise the subject of children. While society expressed prejudice against the illegitimate, it would probably not use the Old Testament language employed by Hester. It is a predictable response, however, from the puritan. While Mrs Arbuthnot is trying to discover what chance Gerald has with Hester, it is also possible that she is torturing herself by leading Hester to express such views aloud. Both women agree, without even discussing it, on one thing – that Gerald can be manipulated into doing what they want. Lady Caroline's remark in pursuing Sir John that 'It is time for him to retire' (p. 82) suggests she is going to put him to bed like a child, and contributes to the comic portrayal of these men as intrinsically infantile.

Gerald's language shows Lord Illingworth's influence – the sneers at Wrockley, the accusations of illogicality and the stress on ambition all echo his father. Mrs Arbuthnot tries to win him by becoming overtly maternal, telling him a story while he sits close like a child at bedtime. Gerald's response surprises her, and perhaps us. The story is so obviously an attempt to make him guess the truth, yet too slow to see it, he parrots smug platitudes of the kind that may well have once been used against Rachel. It is defeat for Mrs Arbuthnot, and only the rapid entrance of Hester saves her from despair. All the strands of the plot converge here. With the line 'He is your own father!' Wilde achieves the **strong curtain** in the penultimate act demanded by the **well-made play** (p. 88).

See **Text 2** of **Extended commentaries** for further discussion of part of this section.

ACT IV

PAGES 88–93

- The following morning, Lady Hunstanton and Mrs Allonby call on Mrs Arbuthnot.
- Gerald announces to the two women that he will not take up the post of Lord Illingworth's secretary.

The action shifts to a new location, Mrs Arbuthnot's sitting-room, with her garden in the background. Gerald is writing a letter when Lady Hunstanton and Mrs Allonby arrive to enquire after his mother – she left the company the previous evening on the excuse of feeling unwell. Gerald says she has not yet come downstairs, and they busy themselves looking around the room, which Lady Hunstanton describes as 'nice and old-fashioned' (p. 89).

CONTEXT

The Victorians were fond of pictures that illustrated an improving moral. William Archer (see **Critical history**) wrote in the *World* that this line – 'He is your own father!' – was so melodramatic it deserved to be a poster or a cheap print to decorate a room.

 CHECK THE BOOK

John Russell Taylor's *The Rise and Fall of the Well Made Play* (1967) usefully discusses the work of Wilde's contemporaries in the theatre and helps to build a picture of the tastes and expectations of a typical audience. He also illustrates the durability of the format with its emphasis on **suspense** and an exciting moment each time the curtain falls.

Gerald tells them that he has given up the secretaryship, considering himself not 'suitable' (p. 91). Both find his decision foolish, and his explanation that he does not want to leave his mother fails to satisfy them. However, they cannot discuss it with Mrs Arbuthnot as the maid enters to say she has a headache and cannot see anyone. Lady Hunstanton remarks, 'if you had a father, Gerald, he wouldn't let you waste your life here' (p. 93). They leave to visit Mrs Daubeny, the Archdeacon's wife. Gerald struggles to complete his letter, complaining that he has 'no right to any name' with which to sign it (p. 93). Mrs Arbuthnot enters just as the ladies pass the French window on their way out of the garden.

COMMENTARY

The shift to a simpler setting is striking after the confrontation in the picture gallery; we might expect to see Mrs Arbuthnot at ease here, and it is a measure of her distress that she is not even up at a time conventionally devoted to visits. It is interesting that in this hotbed of gossip, neither visitor has an inkling of last night's revelations. They inspect her home with curiosity. Lady Hunstanton praises Mrs Arbuthnot's 'good influence' and sees everything in the house as evidence of it (p. 89). Mrs Allonby maintains her usual cynical detachment, but the **irony** of her remark 'I should like to see Lord Illingworth in a happy English home' (p. 89) makes us laugh at rather than with her; the situation is more complex than these patronising sophisticates realise.

The ladies speak in front of Gerald with the same freedom as they did in the all-female company of Act II. Moral judgements here are based on home accessories. Mrs Arbuthnot's goodness is revealed, according to Lady Hunstanton, in 'Fresh natural flowers, books that don't shock one, pictures that one can look at without blushing'. Absent are the 'orchids, foreigners, and French novels' found in women's rooms in London (p. 90). The ladies cheerfully realise their own superficiality as they discuss the pleasures of blushing, and Mrs Allonby admits to affairs with older men. The 'worldly' Gerald, fresh from talking to Lord Illingworth, might have taken this in his stride, but after last night such remarks must seem to him like evidence to support his conclusion that 'I don't want to see the world: I've seen enough of it' (p. 92).

The ladies' exit is a striking piece of theatre: Wilde has them pass the French window as Mrs Arbuthnot enters. It is possible that they catch sight of her at this point. If so, it is evident that they have caught her out in a lie, and they have no information to help them guess why this 'sweet saint' (p. 90) has told it.

See **Text 3** of **Extended commentaries** for further discussion of part of this section.

PAGES 93–7

- Gerald insists that he will order Lord Illingworth to marry his mother, but she refuses.
- Hester enters unobserved.

Gerald explains that he has written to Lord Illingworth asking him to call. Mrs Arbuthnot refuses to meet him, although she is resigned to Gerald taking the secretaryship. Gerald replies that 'Nothing in the world' would make him leave her, and invites her to guess what he has written (p. 94). When she cannot he proudly announces that his letter orders Illingworth to marry her: 'I will make him do it: he will not dare to refuse' (p. 95). Mrs Arbuthnot amazes Gerald by saying that *she* refuses. He explains that although he can gain nothing, it will be 'something' for her. Rapidly, he moves to insisting that she marry Illingworth as a duty to other women; Mrs Arbuthnot rejects this. She thinks she owes nothing to other women, and women like Hester, who have not 'sinned', cannot understand her (p. 97). She will act, she says, for herself alone. Hester quietly slips into the room unobserved.

COMMENTARY

Wilde's first audience would probably have felt reasonably confident about the way this scene would develop. The most popular play of the 1880s, Sir Arthur Pinero's *Sweet Lavender* (1888), showed the reconciliation of a pair of illicit lovers over their

CHECK THE NET

The text of *A Woman of No Importance* is available online at **www.online-literature.com**; this is useful if you wish to search for specific phrases or key words in the play.

child. Even when this did not occur in popular drama, the 'fallen' woman conventionally remained humble and meek. Traditional family values would be asserted with the final curtain. Here Wilde momentarily appears to be turning Gerald into the spokesman for such moralism. Mrs Arbuthnot's line 'But, Gerald, it is I who refuse' (p. 95) would be unexpected enough to provoke a gasp from the audience in the 1890s. Twenty-first-century audiences are better placed to relish the sly comedy in Wilde's presentation of the patronising Gerald announcing his plan for a forced marriage as a sort of treat for his mother.

The pile-up of commas in Gerald's harangue (p. 95) suggests a series of pompous little pauses, each one heralding a more crudely obvious point: 'But surely it will be something for you, that you, my mother' (she hardly needs to be told who she is) 'should, however late' (this verges on rudeness) 'become the wife of the man who is my father' (who hardly needs this coy avoidance of his name in a private context). Despite all the statements in the play that women are irrational, it is Gerald who makes the most spectacularly illogical demand here. Failing to persuade her that the marriage will benefit her, he proclaims with splendid **hyperbole** that she must do it to save 'all the other women in the world, lest he betray more' (p. 96) – as if a philanderer forced into marriage can be reformed by a wedding ring.

While Gerald is comic in this scene, Mrs Arbuthnot is not; her bitterness is more than a statement about the problems of single parenthood. If it implies that other women are *incapable* of offering sympathy or help – a lesson for the approaching Hester? – she also *refuses* it with proud decision: 'my wrongs are my own, and I will bear them alone' (p. 97). It is worth recalling Lady Hunstanton's earlier exit here: she is off to visit Mrs Daubeny, the passive object of her charity – but all her goodwill is reserved for the Archdeacon for putting up with her. Mrs Arbuthnot may be right in her assertion that the double standard operates even in the field of pity.

PAGES 97–103

- Hester overhears Mrs Arbuthnot explain herself to Gerald.
- Hester supports Mrs Arbuthnot in her refusal to marry Lord Illingworth.
- Hester reveals her love for Gerald, and Mrs Arbuthnot gives them her blessing.

While Hester listens, Gerald pushes his demands. He exclaims, 'What mother has ever refused to marry the father of her own child? None' – only to receive a firm reply: 'Let me be the first, then' (p. 97). He moves on to religious argument – his mother must 'believe' a marriage would be right. Mrs Arbuthnot replies that a vow to Illingworth would be a 'lie to God' (p. 98). She complains that men do not understand the meaning of motherhood – a fight against the forces of death, for which sons are never properly grateful. She says she felt unworthy to share the social life Gerald made for himself, but her abstemiousness and good works were not chosen – just her only options. Even so, she does not repent of a sin that gave her Gerald. He is moved, but still presses, and it is Hester who rushes to support her and offer her a home. She tells Gerald to 'Ask your own heart' (p. 101), and he breaks down in tears. Hester admits her love for him to Mrs Arbuthnot, saying her wealth makes no difference. Mrs Arbuthnot leads her to Gerald, declaring: 'I cannot give you a father, but I have brought you a wife' (p. 102). They express the hope that Mrs Arbuthnot will not leave them, and then the young couple go out into the garden together.

COMMENTARY

Two years later, audiences were to laugh at the moment in *The Importance of Being Earnest* when a lady admires a man for undergoing the 'fearful ordeal' of baptism to please her. It is possible that the phrase 'so hideous a sacrifice' used about marrying a rich and witty aristocrat might also have had its comic side for the audience (p. 97). But Mrs Arbuthnot's cry 'Let me be the first' is a genuinely radical moment. In the speeches that follow, the actress playing Mrs Arbuthnot has a tremendous opportunity to establish herself as the central character. The language comes close to the edge of **melodrama** – few Victorian audiences could resist a sentimental **allusion** to religion or to the fragility of childhood – but is used in a highly original way to prevent a simplistic conclusion. Gerald tries to create just that with his appeal to 'the religion that you taught me when I was a boy' (p. 97). However, his mother demands a less mechanistic definition of what binds a man to a woman. In an era painfully navigating early divorce legislation, she comes close, when declaring herself 'too bound' to Illingworth (p. 98), to disparaging the institution of marriage altogether.

Emphasising her sacrifice also makes Mrs Arbuthnot an unattractive figure. But her rhetoric about death is not empty: in the nineteenth century mothers did 'fight with death' (p. 98). Many children, even among the better off, died in infancy; many mothers died of the complications associated with childbirth. There is emotional blackmail in the hint that careless sons should 'repay' the casual hurts they do their mothers (p. 98). Nonetheless, Mrs Arbuthnot is shatteringly honest in her resentment at giving up 'the pleasant things of life' (p. 99). This is not the speech expected of a domestic angel. Illegitimate mothers in nineteenth-century literature could be shown loving their children, but the public expected them to take delight in sacrifice. They were certainly not expected to glory in their status with a ringing cry of 'Child of my shame, be still the child of my shame!' (p. 99). Some critics found this line overblown, but it is short and memorable, a line the audience might discuss at parties.

The sermonising tone of this section is exactly calculated to make Hester's sudden 'conversion' credible. It is explicitly religious; the women share biblical allusions – 'green valleys and fresh waters' (p. 100) is a semi-quotation from Psalm 23 – to stress their rapport. This rapport is also comically visible in their animated discussion over an inert Gerald moaning 'what should I do?' (p. 101). Mrs Arbuthnot seizes a role usually given to a man at the close of a romantic **comedy**. When the enterprising heroine has removed the obstacles, it is usually her father who hands her over to her chosen husband. Here both active roles are played by women; Gerald just sits there.

CONTEXT

Infant mortality rates had begun to improve since 1850, but twenty-five per cent of children failed to reach adulthood in the 1890s. Puerperal fever (also known as childbed fever) accounted for the deaths of between ten and thirty-five per cent of mothers in mid nineteenth-century hospitals.

PAGES 103–12

- Lord Illingworth attempts to make Gerald his heir.
- He offers to marry Mrs Arbuthnot, who refuses and strikes him.
- Gerald and Hester return, and a new family is formed.

Lord Illingworth is announced and enters despite the fact that Mrs Arbuthnot has refused to see him. She coldly points out that Gerald may still attack him. Illingworth shrugs off his behaviour with Hester and makes a proposal: though he cannot legally have the title, Gerald can inherit much of his property; in return he is to live with his father for six months each year. Mrs Arbuthnot replies that Hester will make Gerald financially secure, and they are all going away together.

Illingworth notices the letter addressed to him and says that 'to get my son back' (p. 108) he is willing to marry Mrs Arbuthnot. She rejects him and explains her feelings: 'I have two passions, Lord Illingworth: my love of him, my hate of you' (p. 109). Illingworth cannot believe she has turned Gerald against him; she tells him that was the work of Hester. Illingworth admits defeat, but as a parting shot refers to Rachel and Gerald as 'one's mistress, and one's –' (p. 111). Mrs Arbuthnot strikes him with his glove before he can articulate the word 'bastard', and he leaves in silence. Gerald and Hester return, and Gerald idly picks up the glove and asks who has called. She replies, 'A man of no importance' (p. 112).

COMMENTARY

Lord Illingworth is at a disadvantage from the start; he has to sneak past the maid, only to be spotted in the mirror. Mrs Arbuthnot even speaks with her back to him, a remarkable violation of etiquette. She calls him 'George Harford' (p. 103), while he uses her name far less often than in the persuasive Act II. Interestingly, he is the one to raise the subject of Hester, and he cannot name her either – she is 'That silly Puritan girl', an object in his way (p. 104). Mrs

CONTEXT

Calling cards were part of the ritual of polite visits. Visitors would place cards bearing their names on a tray for the maid so that she could announce them. When Mrs Arbuthnot tells the maid to say she is 'not at home' she is using the standard polite formula to indicate that she is not available to callers. When she amends this to 'Say I will not see him' (p. 103) she is administering a severe snub – and does not mind the maid knowing this.

QUESTION

Herbert Beerbohm Tree had no qualms about cutting lines he felt were controversial. If you were directing a production of *A Woman of No Importance* today, are there lines you might choose to omit? Why?

Arbuthnot's comment 'A kiss may ruin a human life' makes it clear she does not believe his version of events (p. 104). She cannot believe that he is more responsible now than he was in his twenties.

Illingworth changes tack rapidly, and he speaks with a sharp awareness of the legal situation. He cannot, ever, make Gerald legitimate. If the law is unreasonable, however, he also seems happy for Gerald to be one of the class who maintain such laws: 'What more can a gentleman desire in this world?' (p. 105). Mrs Arbuthnot's sarcastic retort, 'Nothing more, I am quite sure', turns the exchange into an overt class confrontation. She treats Illingworth as he once treated her by considering the relationship in purely financial terms, pointing out that Gerald no longer needs his money. This leaves Illingworth no grounds of appeal but those of affection: he wants Gerald. Ironically, his patronising proposal of marriage employs language similar to Mrs Arbuthnot's when explaining to Gerald why she would refuse him – for her, marriage would be 'sacrifice' (p. 97); for Illingworth, it is 'surrender' (p. 108). His condescending tone makes credible the violence of her assertion that she hates him and that the hate is bound to 'the sort of love I have for Gerald' (p. 109).

This is a bold stroke at such a point in the play. The audience probably expects a happy ending. But there is a sense that, although the outcome may still be beneficent, conforming to the ideal of the penitent single mother has permanently warped Mrs Arbuthnot. For the first time, though, she verges on wit in her triumphant repetition of Lord Illingworth's own **epigrams** about children, who 'begin by loving their parents' but 'Rarely, if ever ... forgive them' (p. 110). Illingworth's recovery is awkward, and some critics have felt his descent into the clumsy sneers of farewell is out of character. However, it may indicate that he is genuinely shaken. His parting shot creates an exciting climax: the censorship of the time would never, as the audience well knew, permit anyone to utter the word 'bastard' on the stage. They are allowed a shock, as the actor seems about to break a major taboo. Then they have an equally powerful moment of relief: not only is the taboo maintained (and the villain punished), but the seal is set on Mrs Arbuthnot's respectability by letting her cut off the forbidden word.

The energy of this dialogue confirms that something has been accomplished. Now her bitterness has been articulated, Mrs Arbuthnot can change. With the entry of Gerald and Hester we have the image of 'a man and a woman in a garden' (as mentioned in Act I, p. 31), but this time there will be no fall. Instead, there is a new family. As Mrs Arbuthnot picks up and changes the title line of the play, she again draws near to a kind of humour. Unmarried, defiant, she ushers in a fresh and better world.

EXTENDED COMMENTARIES

TEXT 1 – ACT II, PAGES 57–62

From 'So that is our son' to 'I will not let him go.'

Lord Illingworth has asked to talk privately with Mrs Arbuthnot; everyone is delighted to ensure that he can do so. Gerald anticipates that all her reservations about the secretaryship will disappear. The rest of the company (with the possible exception of Hester) are sure that she will want a chance to express her gratitude properly. But the audience has been expecting this moment since the curtain fell on Act I.

So far the stage has thronged with life. Suddenly there are only two people talking quietly. We have the sudden sense that we are eavesdropping. This is appropriate, because in this world of privileged landowners there is very little genuine privacy: everyone is constantly on display. The scene is accompanied throughout by the sound of Hester's violin drifting in from the music-room. While this adds poignancy to an encounter between former lovers, it also acts as a reminder that the whole company is in the next room and may interrupt at any moment. Mrs Arbuthnot will have only a fleeting space in which to think and decide her son's future.

Lord Illingworth confirms what many of the audience will have already guessed: 'So that is our son, Rachel!' (p. 57). His use of her Christian name establishes a tone of quiet familiarity, befitting the affection he evidently feels for his son; but by the end of this

> **CONTEXT**
>
> The critic William Archer described this confrontation scene as 'the most virile and intelligent piece of English dramatic writing of our day ... There is no situation-hunting, no posturing ... There is nothing conventional in it, nothing insincere. In a word, it is a piece of adult art' (quoted in *Oscar Wilde: The Critical Heritage*, edited by Karl Beckson, 1970, p. 145).

CHECK THE NET

The Victorian Web – **www.victorian web.org** – examines aspects of Victorian literature, history and culture. For a more specific look at Wilde himself, click on Authors and Oscar Wilde.

episode he has used the name more than ten times, suggesting that he is trying to force this upon her. Right from the outset, he assumes that he has already got his own way: 'The world will know him merely as my private secretary, but to me he will be something very near' (p. 58). This smoothly authoritative attitude suggests a practised seducer rather than the innocent boy he claims to have been 'when the whole thing began in your father's garden' (p. 58). For him, as Act I has shown, gardens are not **symbolic** of innocence but of sexual desire, a backdrop for his flirtation with Mrs Allonby and his plot to kiss Hester. While Mrs Arbuthnot's accusations are couched in the overblown language of **melodrama**, she is undoubtedly – like most heroines of Victorian melodrama – a genuine victim of a rigid class structure and sexual double standards. Illingworth refuses to consider the past from the woman's point of view at all; for him the only interests to be consulted are those of father and son.

The scene is notable for the intensity of the focus on the absent Gerald. The words 'my' and 'mine' are applied with great frequency, and after the opening line the word 'our' is used only to score a point. Lord Illingworth cuts off Mrs Arbuthnot's account of her twenty years of 'suffering' and 'shame' quite callously (p. 60); similarly, she expresses no interest at all in what has happened to him since they parted. Despite this careful avoidance of the subject, however, we are given indications of the strength of that old passion. Illingworth's earlier tribute to Mrs Arbuthnot's beauty and the sheer energy of her diatribes once she sheds her initial coldness create a sexual tension that charges the scene with life. This is a special relationship: both characters behave quite differently with each other from the way they behave with anyone else. They seem to have less command over their language. Illingworth may imagine that he is presenting logical arguments by employing phrases such as 'the common-sense point of view', contrasting his behaviour with Mrs Arbuthnot's 'illogical' attitude and accusing her of talking 'sentimentally', but his grumpy insult 'typical woman' has an odd note of intimacy (pp. 60–1). Briefly, the conversation sounds like a row between an old married couple. It is one of the rare times we are impelled to laugh at him rather than at his witty remarks.

The chilly, negative Mrs Arbuthnot catches fire as she speaks for the first time at length and at speed, concluding in a flurry of biblical references describing Gerald as 'the little vineyard of my life … the walled-in garden and the well of water; the ewe-lamb God sent me' (p. 62). Biblical language, of course, fits the pillar of the church described in Act I. However, the vineyard and the walled garden come from the Song of Solomon, a lover's description of his beloved. The 'ewe lamb' is also remarkably unsuitable: it **alludes** to King David's forbidden desire for Bathsheba. All of these images are comically inappropriate to the hearty enthusiastic 'chap' who has bounded round the drawing-room forcing this reluctant pair together. Mrs Arbuthnot is, perhaps, unconsciously trying to forget that her son is a grown man.

This lack of control by both characters makes it clear that they have a unique capacity to hurt each other. It makes them both seem more human. If this is a dispute between parents, between members of different classes and between lovers, it is also a dispute about the meaning of family by a son and a daughter. The careful placing of the characters in their own family context is one of the factors that give the scene the 'adult' quality praised by William Archer. Rather than running the gamut of stock emotions for a typical confrontation between 'fallen' woman and seducer, Wilde shows some of the forces which individualise their response to the situation. Illingworth appears to be the product of a loveless marriage riven by disagreements; there is considerable **irony** in the way he complains of being dominated by his mother. While this may account for some of his misogynist sentiments in this scene, it is clear that he still shares some of his aristocratic mother's disregard for women of an inferior class. Mrs Arbuthnot, on the other hand, speaks only of her father, as if she was raised by a single parent and is replicating the only experience of parenting she understands. Illingworth's warning – 'Children begin by loving their parents. After a time they judge them. Rarely, if ever, do they forgive them' (pp. 61–2) – is a deft summary of the danger in which he will place Mrs Arbuthnot if she does not give in to him. But it also has a broader application in the world of the play: to Gerald's parents, and to their parents in turn.

? QUESTION

In Act III Mrs Arbuthnot declares: 'I think there are many things women should never forgive' (p. 76). Examine the role of forgiveness in the play.

TEXT 2 – ACT III, PAGES 85–8

From 'Gerald, come near to me' to the end of Act III.

Mrs Arbuthnot has tried a number of different strategies to dissuade
Gerald from becoming Lord Illingworth's secretary. First she
expressed practical doubts about his ability; then she confronted
Illingworth directly. Gerald has now had a long talk with the
persuasive Illingworth and she is taking one last chance to talk him
out of it. This fresh attempt is bolstered by Hester's confidence in
her. However, their recent conversation has made it clear that there
is no hope of marriage between puritan Hester and illegitimate
Gerald. The situation is made more urgent by Gerald's response
to his mother's straightforward plea, a response in language so like
Illingworth's that her efforts seem hopeless. To tell her own story is
dangerous – Gerald may reject her – and her willingness to risk this
shows her desperation. She begins by stressing her maternal role,
drawing him close like 'a little boy … mother's own boy' while she
runs her fingers through his hair (p. 85). It is a touching image, but
also slightly disturbing; she will not treat Gerald as an adult over a
matter that profoundly concerns him.

Her **narrative** starts in simple language. We almost hear the voice of
the young Rachel in short, broken sentences such as 'She loved him
so much, and he had promised to marry her!' (p. 86). The plainness
of this story is touching and direct. Both Mrs Arbuthnot and the
audience imagine Gerald will grasp its significance and make his
mother's task easier by asking her outright – is it her own life she is
telling him about? The language changes, however. It becomes more
like a moral tract or a speech from a **melodrama**. There is repetition
to drive the point home – 'her life was ruined, and her soul ruined,
and all that was sweet, and good, and pure in her ruined also' – and
exaggerated **imagery**: 'no anodyne can give her sleep! no poppies
forgetfulness!' She seems to have forgotten her son in the process
of luxuriating in her own grief. If Gerald was slow on the uptake
earlier, he could be forgiven for failing to recognise his mother in
this description of 'a woman who wears a mask, like a thing that is
a leper' (p. 86). His brisk reply, 'it all sounds very tragic, of course',
is a dreadful blow to the woman nerving herself up for her great

**CHECK
THE BOOK**

*Nineteenth Century
Plays*, edited by
George Rowell
(1972), provides a
selection of popular
melodramas of the
period.

disclosure. Nonetheless, it can be a comic moment for the audience. It briefly breaks the tension before Gerald articulates his bluff and uncomprehendingly masculine perspective that 'No nice girl' would behave like that (p. 86).

The pause that follows is charged with dramatic possibilities. The audience will probably be judging both the mother for her self-centredness and the son for his smugness. Nevertheless, a real struggle is taking place in Mrs Arbuthnot, and the outcome is unpredictable until the very moment she speaks. The decision to let Gerald go implies that she judges herself more harshly than the audience or the characters could. It might also, depending on the way the line is spoken, indicate a degree of disappointment in her son. The entrance of Hester with Illingworth in pursuit just as he is proclaiming that Illingworth is not 'capable of anything infamous or base' certainly tells us all we need to know about Gerald as a judge of character (p. 87).

We never see Lord Illingworth's assault on Hester. Has he merely tried to snatch a kiss to fulfil the wager? Or is her extreme reaction provoked by a more extreme situation? Certainly she takes it for granted that Gerald will protect her, and he does so in a highly melodramatic style. As he shouts about insults to 'a thing as pure as my own mother' (p. 87), Mrs Arbuthnot, raw from the decision not to confess her own sexual slip in the wake of that remark about a 'nice girl', must find the situation extraordinarily painful. Her face, and Illingworth's, will be showing some complex emotions.

This complexity plays against the melodrama of the situation itself. It was common for a play of the period to bring down the curtain on a stunning revelation of paternity, and some critics accused Wilde of resorting to a cheap trick. A witty **parody** in the *Theatre* for June 1893 interprets the play in the light of melodramatic conventions:

> GERALD   Villain! (*Gallery wakes up*) … I propose to thrash you within an inch of your life (*gallery wide awake and expectant*) so clear a ring, mother, and hold my coat.

CONTEXT

The real-life story of the murder of Maria Marten in Suffolk in 1827 provoked huge public interest. Plays were written and performed during the trial; the anonymous *Maria Marten or The Murder in the Red Barn* was a sensational hit and became one of the most frequently performed melodramas of the nineteenth century.

MRS ARBUTHNOT (*To herself*) Now for an effective curtain. (*With pardonable pride*) This, I think, is *my* situation.

GERALD (*Squaring up to Lord Illingworth*) Come on!

MRS ARBUTHNOT (*Throwing herself between them in the approved fashion*) Gerald, forbear! If thou wouldst strike anything, let it be an attitude, for he, Lord Illingworth, is thy father! (*Sensation, group, and curtain*)

However, this information is a surprise to Gerald, not to us, and we are free to consider its implications more soberly. The scene does not end, as many of its contemporaries did, with a **tableau** of actors frozen in heroic postures for the audience to relish the power of the moment. Instead, Wilde's stage directions are detailed. Mrs Arbuthnot sinks to her knees '*in shame*', and '*After a time*' Gerald raises her up, puts his arm round her and leads her away (p. 88). Wilde seems to be subverting the convention in order to stress that we cannot escape real problems with the fall of a curtain. Gerald has to grasp his new status and make a decision in the light of it. What he chooses to do, sharply jolted out of the religiosity he has learned from his mother and the cynicism he has absorbed from his father, is to hold his mother voluntarily for the first time in the play. Nobody, in the last moment of this act, is allowed to 'strike an attitude' without realising that life still has to go on after the moment of striking it.

TEXT 3 – ACT IV, PAGES 88–91

From the start of Act IV to 'My dear, you really mustn't talk like that in this house.'

Act IV begins quietly after the dramatic conclusion to Act III, when Mrs Arbuthnot prevented Gerald attacking Lord Illingworth by revealing his parentage. The curtain rises on the lonely figure writing at the table; this may continue for a few minutes before the entry of the maid, so that the audience can wonder how Gerald feels about his situation in the light of day. The arrival of Lady Hunstanton and Mrs Allonby indicates that the smooth surface of the community has not been disturbed. Their call is one of the routine politenesses of their class. Mrs Arbuthnot would normally be expected to be 'at home' to visitors at this time, and politeness dictates that they must stay a little while in case she is able to see them.

Their inspection of the room is a piece of **stage business** that probably continues throughout much of the dialogue, even when they are not talking directly about what they see. They are basically entertaining themselves during what they may consider a fairly boring visit – but their curiosity also allows Wilde to bring to our attention the differences between this setting and the grandeur of Hunstanton Chase. There is scope for a designer to show the character of Mrs Arbuthnot and also to provide **properties** which the ladies can pick up and examine. There is considerable comedy in their different responses – while Lady Hunstanton is benevolent, Mrs Allonby peers through a lorgnette, an action which forces the actress to hold her head high and prompts a superior expression.

Arthur Conan Doyle had already begun publishing his Sherlock Holmes stories. His famous detective draws all kinds of conclusions from detailed observation of ordinary household objects, and there is a little discreet detective work going on here. Both women agree that the room suggests 'a happy English home' (p. 89); but there is perhaps a **subtext** to their discussion. As they are clearly unaware of last night's confrontation, why does Mrs Allonby now bring Lord Illingworth into the conversation? Is it possible that she still feels both jealousy and curiosity about 'the lady in black velvet' (Act II, p. 56) who has occupied so much of his attention? Perhaps she quotes one of Illingworth's **paradoxes** – 'a good influence is the worst in the world' (p. 89) – to emphasise to herself and Lady Hunstanton that there is nothing between Lord Illingworth and Mrs Arbuthnot.

Lady Hunstanton's declaration that it would do Illingworth 'a great deal of good' to be brought into this 'happy English home' (p. 89) may contain a little barb: 'Most women in London, nowadays, seem to furnish their rooms with nothing but orchids, foreigners, and French novels' (pp. 89–90). Is this a gentle reproach to the woman who took Illingworth to see the 'orchid … as beautiful as the seven

CONTEXT

A lorgnette was a pair of spectacles or opera glasses mounted on a single stem at the side. Mrs Allonby may be too vain to wear spectacles.

CONTEXT

Arthur Conan Doyle (1859–1930) first introduced Sherlock Holmes to the English reading public in 1887, in the story *A Study in Scarlet.* The detective appeared in numerous stories printed in the *Strand Magazine*; these were published together in a number of collections, the first of which, *The Adventures of Sherlock Holmes,* was published a year before the first performance of *A Woman of No Importance.*

CHECK THE BOOK

The American playwright Susan Glaspell (1882–1948), a near contemporary of Wilde's, wrote a short play, *Trifles* (1916), in which women inspect small domestic items in the room of a woman accused of murdering her vicious husband, and deduce that she has been driven to it after he killed her songbird.

deadly sins' (Act I, p. 20)? Mrs Allonby is certainly equal to it. As Lady Hunstanton enumerates the evidence of Mrs Arbuthnot's virtue: 'Fresh natural flowers, books that don't shock one, pictures that one can look at without blushing', Mrs Allonby's retort – 'But I like blushing' – is not just witty and decisive, it directs the conversation into risqué generalities rather than current relationships (p. 90). When Mrs Allonby next returns to the subject of Lord Illingworth, it is in a more frivolous vein. She is plainly beginning to flirt with Gerald when she remarks, 'I wish Lord Illingworth would ask me to be his secretary.' This prompts Lady Hunstanton to rein her in: 'you really mustn't talk like that in this house' (p. 91).

PART THREE

CRITICAL APPROACHES

CHARACTERISATION

In his story about art and the theatre, *The Portrait of Mr W. H.*, Wilde complained that the critics of his day had an unfortunate tendency to make an 'over-realistic identification of the actor with his role' (Folio edition, p. 461). Victorian literature tended to assume that a well-drawn character would be one of profound psychological depth, a figure who could be interpreted and discussed as if he or she were a real person. Wilde, however, preferred the audience to be continually aware that they were watching actors playing their parts, because his plays were vitally concerned with the business of self-presentation. Wilde's audience were bound by a code of manners; there were topics they could not discuss, emotions they could not display and information they could not reveal – but they could nonetheless communicate these things through a careful choice of vocabulary or **body language**.

Such codes operated to allow upper-class society to function smoothly; in this exclusive circle it was important to play your part well. Wilde's characters were designed to let the audience recognise themselves on stage and enjoy their own artifice. He once made this quite explicit by stepping on stage at the fall of the curtain to congratulate them on their performance. He also worked closely with the people who produced and performed in his plays and would sometimes craft a character to fit an actor's talents. Sometimes they did this for themselves – not always to Wilde's satisfaction. The characters in *A Woman of No Importance* should be understood as vehicles for experienced actors. They are not fixed entities but opportunities to make choices: to emphasise or play down a particular trait, to inflect a line and give it one meaning rather than another, even to make a gesture or adopt an expression which suggests that what the character *says* in the text is not necessarily what he or she *thinks*. This fluidity gives Wilde's plays their continuing vitality: a new generation of performers will inevitably find fresh choices to make, and the characters will gain a fresh relevance.

CONTEXT

The Portrait of Mr W. H. can be found in Holland's 1994 *Complete Works of Oscar Wilde* (p. 1180). A fascinating mix of critical essay and short story, it outlines an elaborate fantasy about a boy actor beloved of Shakespeare who inspires the sonnets, and a critic who forges material to prove that this was actually true.

In this section the characters are discussed in order of their appearance in the play.

LADY CAROLINE

Lady Caroline speaks with absolute authority on every topic from entertainment for the poor to the appropriate marital status for an ambassador, and does not expect to hear contradictory opinions. She appears to subscribe to a rigid moral code, condemning the 'love of pleasure amongst the upper classes' (Act I, p. 19), and constantly enquires about the conduct of people such as Mrs Allonby in order to condemn them. However, she hypocritically overlooks the notorious debauchery of her brother, because 'he has one of the best cooks in London' (Act II, p. 47). She has an exhaustive knowledge of her exclusive society, able to recite family histories from memory – including income and inheritance. She is also adamant that working for a living is 'not considered the thing' (Act I, p. 7). She relentlessly polices her husband's relationships, and disrupts important conversations in chase of him. For example she charges into an emotive scene between Hester and Mrs Arbuthnot in Act III (p. 82) – a fact to which her lack of consideration for others makes her completely oblivious. Indeed, it is tempting to see Lady Caroline as Wilde's living illustration of Illingworth's joke about 'the unspeakable in full pursuit of the uneatable' (Act I, p. 19). While her jealousy is a running joke, the social power that she wields is not; fortunately, her insensitivity means that, like the other ladies, she misses out on the revelations about Mrs Arbuthnot.

HESTER

Hester is the youngest person at the house party and, as an orphan, a woman and a foreigner, she is the most vulnerable. Her name is the same as that of the heroine of *The Scarlet Letter*, Nathaniel Hawthorne's famous 1850 novel about a woman who has an illegitimate child in the harsh Puritan community of New England in the seventeenth century. She is herself a New Englander; but at the start of the play at least, she resembles those who persecute her namesake rather than the courageous unmarried mother herself. She is a patriotic American, expressing her love of the American countryside and of a value system that has the greatest 'respect'

CONTEXT

Hester is called Mabel in early drafts of the play, but Wilde wanted 'some nice New England name' and chose to call her after the heroine of *The Scarlet Letter*. A dramatisation of Hawthorne's novel had recently been seen on the London stage. It is a sly **irony** that Wilde calls his 'Puritan' after the sinner of the piece, and gives his amoral **dandy** a name like that of the most self-righteous character, the cold and implacable husband Chillingworth.

(Act I, p. 8) for those who work for a living. She believes in social equality, declaring that America has 'no lower classes' (Act II, p. 43), and certainly does not hold it against Gerald that he has no money. She also believes in equality between the sexes. She can express her admiration for Gerald on short acquaintance, and at the end of the play tells his mother that she will marry him. (He may have expressed the desire to propose to her, but does not appear to have done so yet.)

Her idea of sexual morality is conservative. She certainly despises the double standard which allows men like Lord Henry to be 'asked everywhere' while 'those whose ruin is due to him' are treated as outcasts (Act II, p. 45). However, she believes in equality of punishment rather than a change in outlook, and her ideas about retribution do not seem very different from those displayed in *The Scarlet Letter*. Her language is strongly influenced by the Bible – as was that of the characters in Hawthorne's novel – and in particular by the Old Testament, which lays emphasis on the punishment of sins. She expresses herself with the force and fluency of a public orator or a preacher; she may well be a member of an organisation which encourages her to make speeches. In the play she makes them at inappropriate moments – but this reflects the fact that she is extremely young and perhaps feels too shy to handle casual chatter. She is taken aback by the discussion of the Ideal Man when the women are at coffee in Act II, saying she does not 'believe that any women could really hold such views of life' (p. 42). Lady Hunstanton's kind reassurance that she is right seems to confuse her even more; she cannot understand why people might choose to be playful rather than truthful. We never see her in a playful moment herself.

However, Hester can be quite witty in her own defence. 'The English aristocracy supply us with our curiosities,' she retorts to Mrs Allonby's barbed remark about American manners (Act II, p. 43). Her accusation that 'if you throw bread to the poor, it is merely to keep them quiet' suggests that she has a real interest in politics (Act II, p. 44). Wilde may slyly imply that she takes her father's millions and her Paris frocks for granted, but only Lord Illingworth matches her articulacy on behalf of the poor.

> **CONTEXT**
>
> Hawthorne (1804–64) was born in Salem, Massachusetts, and worked in the custom house there, an experience he describes in the preface to *The Scarlet Letter*. He wrote a number of novels and short stories, including *The House of the Seven Gables* (1851).

CONTEXT

In contrast to Mr Kelvil's sentimental praise of 'Purity' as a feminine virtue, the social purity movement of the 1890s was driven by women. They were anxious to remove prostitutes looking for customers around public houses and **music halls**, and to censor some of the more risqué popular songs of the day. At the heart of the movement was a concern about the growing incidence of syphilis in wives who risked being infected by straying husbands – the government's only attempt to address this issue had been the notorious 1864 Contagious Diseases Act, which treated women themselves as the source of the problem.

Uncomfortably aware of her outsider status, Hester turns to Mrs Arbuthnot for reassurance that 'A woman who has sinned should be punished, shouldn't she?' (Act III, p. 80).

However, Hester does change. This is not the 'conversion' accomplished by the plot between Mrs Allonby and Lord Illingworth – at least not in the way they intend. She responds to his kiss with terror. This is partly because its **motivation** is cruel. But it also suggests that she is extremely inexperienced and that all her pronouncements about the way men and women behave are gathered from books rather than real life. Her meeting with a real 'fallen' woman is the real stimulus for change; she ceases to think in terms of 'A woman who has sinned' and has to make a judgement about someone she already likes and respects. Her admission that 'I was wrong. God's law is only Love' (Act IV, p. 102) is gracious, and of all the characters she has travelled furthest.

SIR JOHN

Sir John has very little chance to say anything apart from 'I am quite comfortable' (Act I, p. 11) when Lady Caroline fusses around him with overshoes and shawls in order to peel him away from a female guest. His role, nevertheless, is more significant than the number of his lines might indicate. It offers the actor a chance to make a comic comment on the action through **body language**. He can choose to play Sir John as a meek little man. On the other hand, he can adopt a calm demeanour to indicate that he serenely ignores Lady Caroline if he wants to enjoy the company of women – and that the guests cooperate in helping him avoid her (Act III, p. 73). He can apparently be very animated on the subject of Patagonia when allowed to speak, and it is through his facial expression – taking pride in a harmless hobby or delighting in some shocking secret knowledge? – that we deduce the implications of Mrs Allonby's remark that Patagonians do 'everything' (Act III, p. 74).

LADY HUNSTANTON

Lady Hunstanton is the hostess of the country-house party where the play is set, and has selected all the guests. Not everyone approves of the way she 'mixes' (Act I, p. 6), but she has considerable power and influence and exercises these with a kind heart. She has invited Gerald specifically to meet Lord Illingworth in order to advance his career. She is at pains to ensure that the company all get on well, bringing Hester into the conversation when she seems to be left out. She also controls the emotional temperature of the conversation: when Mrs Arbuthnot says, bitterly, that 'The ruin of another woman's life' (Act III, p. 76) is an unforgivable act, she adroitly shifts the conversation into generalities.

What makes Lady Hunstanton an entertaining comic character is the way she constantly collapses serious moral issues and trivialities into one another. She remarks to her guests that she had hoped Lord Illingworth would marry Lady Kelso: 'But I believe he said her family was too large. Or was it her feet?' (Act I, p. 10). This may indicate that she is rather muddle-headed; but this refusal to pass serious judgement on anyone allows her to be friends with people as diverse as Mrs Allonby and Mrs Arbuthnot, and to enjoy the social scene to the full. She does, as she puts it, 'take things very, very easily' (Act III, p. 76).

However, if she chooses, the actress playing Lady Hunstanton can give her flashes of intelligence and malice. For instance, when Mrs Allonby snubs the company by saying she is leaving to look at the stars, Lady Hunstanton's reply may be taken at face value, or it may indicate a warning not to carry her flirtations too far. 'You will find a great many, dear, a great many. But don't catch cold' (Act II, p. 48). We may well find ourselves laughing *with* Lady Hunstanton rather than *at* her.

GERALD

Everybody likes Gerald. The pious Hester considers that he has 'a beautiful nature' (Act I, p. 8); the easy-going Lady Hunstanton goes out of her way to help his career; Lord Illingworth is impressed with him – though Gerald calls himself an 'awful duffer' (Act II, p. 55) – even before he realises that Gerald is his son; the cynical Mrs Allonby finds him 'very nice indeed' (Act I, p. 27), and her final demand for a present from India suggests that she would like to continue the flirtation (Act IV, p. 93). This may seem strange in view of the fact that Gerald has almost no personality. He absorbs

CONTEXT

The University of Bristol Theatre Collection contains the prompt copy for the original production of *A Woman of No Importance*. This script used by the stage management contains complete details of everything that happened in the production – including the layout of the stage, the positioning of the actors and details of **stage business**. It makes clear where Wilde's original text was cut or altered. Careful reading of a prompt copy allows us to gain some sense of performances given before the days of film or digital recording.

? **QUESTION**

'Children begin by loving their parents. After a time they judge them. Rarely, if ever, do they forgive them' (Act II, pp. 61–2 and Act IV, p. 110). Do you think this is an accurate account of Gerald's emotional journey in the play?

CONTEXT

The first Gerald was Fred Terry (1863–1933), known as one of the handsomest men in the profession, and the handsomest of the acting dynasty of the Terrys. His sister was Ellen Terry, and John Gielgud his nephew. Fred Terry toured England with his own company in a series of swashbuckling dramas in which he played roles like the Scarlet Pimpernel, rescuing aristocratic maidens in distress.

and reflects the ideas of whomever he is with – so much so that his speech constantly alters. After a long talk with Illingworth he sounds like a full-blown aesthete, describing society as 'exquisite' (Act III, p. 84); but he still uses the language of Old Testament morality absorbed from his mother when they argue and he demands: 'Atonement must be made' (Act IV, p. 95). When life is going smoothly he takes on some of Hester's decisiveness and initiates their first time alone together in Act I. When it is not, he flounders, asking Hester repeatedly: 'what shall I do? (Act IV, p. 100). He is finally silenced altogether, weeping on the sofa, when none of his previous experiences seem to equip him to deal with the situation.

This lack of distinguishing characteristics, however, makes Gerald a credible object of desire; others can project their views onto him and are then touched by the energy and enthusiasm with which he responds. His function in the dramatic structure is to be what was known as the **jeune premier**: the young male lead whose love of the young female lead, or **ingénue**, will occupy much of the story. Wilde could be confident that the magnetism of an attractive young actor would make Gerald acceptable to the audience. Gerald endears himself to the audience not because of what he is, but because of what happens to him. Not only does he court and win a beautiful girl as a dramatic hero should, but he is faced with complex emotional dilemmas. Everyone could understand the shock of discovering that both his parents are completely different from his childhood image of them – and are seriously at odds now. Gerald, despite his pomposity, does declare a silent solidarity with his mother when she is in despair; at the end of Act III he *'raises his mother up'* (p. 88). He is still passive enough to let the women in his life settle his future at the end of the play. However, his notion that he is 'not worthy' of either of them (Act IV, p. 102) suggests that the shocks he has encountered have made him rethink his values for himself.

MRS ALLONBY

The first Mrs Allonby was Maud Tree (née Helen Maud Holt), whose star status ensured that the audience immediately understood her to be a major character, despite the fact that she has a relatively minor function in the plot. Her link with Lord Illingworth suggests that the audience is encouraged to compare and contrast Mrs Allonby and Mrs Arbuthnot. Although they are in many ways opposites, this is not a simple contrast of 'good' and 'evil'. What makes Mrs Allonby such an original dramatic creation is her self-sufficiency. Unlike the conventional 'bad' woman of a society drama she does not get her comeuppance. She flouts the rules and does not have to suffer the usual consequences of social ostracism or heartbreak. She is well aware of the possibility that there are dangers, but this is part of the attraction of rule-breaking. She remarks that 'to elope is cowardly. It's running away from danger. And danger has become so rare in modern life' (Act I, p. 12). Her reputation might severely damage a more timid woman; she survives in society partly because she is 'very well born' (Act I, p. 7) and because she manages to keep precise details of her misdemeanours unknown. Even Lady Caroline, with the marriage market at her fingertips, is not sure whether Mrs Allonby has allowed more than her 'clever tongue' to 'run away' with her and if she is still in the habit (Act I, p. 21). This is not because she is discreet in the usual sense of the word; she makes remarks such as 'I delight in men over seventy. They always offer one the devotion of a lifetime' (Act IV, p. 90).

However, these remarks give pleasure to those around her and that may be their primary purpose. Lady Hunstanton says, 'How clever you are, my dear! You never mean a single word you say' (Act II, p. 41). It is the style of Mrs Allonby's discourse, rather than her opinions, that society values, and it is to style rather than to a particular opinion or way of life that she is committed. When she is alone with Lord Illingworth he remarks, 'the button has come off your foil', and she replies, 'I have still the mask' (Act I, p. 31). This mask only occasionally slips to reveal her irritation with Hester – and it is Hester's refusal to wear a mask that annoys her most. Almost everything Mrs Allonby says is calculated to divert or shock an audience. Lady Tree was an accomplished comic actress, and Mrs Allonby's speeches all require precise timing and the ability to hold a stage. When she is holding forth about the failings of her square-chinned Ernest, or the Ideal Man who should 'talk to us as if we were goddesses, and treat us as if we were children' (Act II, p. 39),

CONTEXT

Helen Maud Holt (1864–1937), a lively comedienne, married Herbert Beerbohm Tree in 1883 and often played opposite him. Their daughters Iris and Viola worked with them and were also on the board of Tree's Royal Academy of Dramatic Art (RADA), which he founded in 1904.

CHECK THE FILM

Suri Krishnamma's 1994 film *A Man of No Importance* stars Albert Finney as a bus conductor determined to stage a production of Wilde's *Salomé* and finding the courage to come out in a rural community. The relationship in the film between 'importance', or at least 'individual expression', and an acceptance of dissident sexuality makes its title a fitting one.

CONTEXT

The seven deadly sins are pride, anger, lust, envy, avarice, gluttony and sloth – arguably all committed in the play.

she is not articulating deep personal emotions about sexual frustration or the confinements of domesticity. She is acknowledging the pressures created on men and women alike by the conventions of upper-class marriages grounded in property rather than affection. Her listeners on the stage know these pressures well; so would those in the auditorium.

If Mrs Allonby holds the floor at Hunstanton Chase, she does so by using the techniques of an actress. She does not actually acknowledge the audience beyond the **fourth wall**, but her speeches are not so different from those of a sophisticated **music-hall** performer, the forerunner of a stand-up comedienne. For both the Hunstanton Chase and the West End audience, hearing the rules of society mocked by a charming and elegant figure would have been an enjoyable safety valve. Her mockery may at times slip into the more active pursuit of 'playing with fire' (Act I, p. 12), but 'play' remains the operative word. Mrs Allonby goes with Lord Illingworth to look at an orchid 'as beautiful as the seven deadly sins' (Act I, p. 20). A hot-house flower is an apt **metaphor** for her. The only flirtation she indulges in during the play is with Lord Illingworth, and it proves her to be his intellectual equal, subtle enough to read a smile or casual **allusion** and always able to top a witty remark. They return constantly to trading wit; while in many **comedies** wit is a form of courtship, here it seems to act as a substitute for sex rather than as a prelude to it. Both seem reluctant to begin an affair that will have to end.

Nonetheless, her demand that he kiss 'the Puritan' (Act I, p. 31) seems to bring in elements of spite and voyeurism. Wilde never shows her reaction to what happens in Act III. But it may be that Mrs Allonby, for all her intelligence, can only function in this tightly enclosed world. The 'Puritan' Hester stands not just for innocence, but for a different kind of society. Mrs Allonby would not fit there, but nor is she interested in creating a better one for herself. In the end, she is trapped in a static world that refuses to change – although she is entirely capable of amusing herself in the trap.

LADY STUTFIELD

Lady Stutfield is a sexual optimist. She is single-minded in her determination to capture a lover. Clearly she has learned that it helps to be a good listener. All her conversations with men express enthusiastic interest and agreement, whether the subject is purity or debt. She is persistent; the news that Mr Kelvil is married does put her off her stride, but his later remark to her that 'The secret of life is to resist temptation' suggests that she has tried her luck anyway (Act III, p. 76). She feels no guilt, since she can see a 'very, very sad expression in the eyes of so many married men' (Act II, p. 34). She also tries to captivate Lord Alfred and Lord Illingworth; Illingworth virtually admits that his remark 'Women kneel so gracefully' is made about Lady Stutfield (Act I, p. 25), but leaves us no wiser as to whether she has succeeded.

Her conversations with women tend to lament the cruelties and betrayals of the opposite sex; this is perhaps not so much a deeply held conviction as part of her pose of helplessness. Her distinctive speech pattern, with its 'very, very', suggests a slight breathlessness that will make her look fragile and in need of male protection. She is fascinated by Mrs Allonby, who seems to express her own thought processes for her: 'very, very helpful', she murmurs after their conversation about 'playing with fire' (Act I, p. 12). She does not have much interest in anything other than relationships, reproving Hester's speech about poverty with 'I don't think one should know of these things' (Act II, p. 44). It seems that the major events of the house party pass her by; she is not among those who call on Mrs Arbuthnot the following day. However, the last time we see her, she is disappearing with Sir John, while Lady Caroline charges off in the wrong direction. It may be that Lady Stutfield finally gets what she came for.

MR KELVIL

Mr Kelvil is a Member of Parliament, a powerful man who constantly draws attention to that fact; his pomposity makes him a comic figure. He does not so much discuss subjects as disparage the views of others – as long as they are not in the room. His conversation is so discreetly tailored not to offend that we never

QUESTION

Wilde wrote to the actor Oswald Yorke (1866–1943), who was hoping for a role in the first production, that *A Woman of No Importance* had few male parts and defined it as 'a woman's play'. Was this just a polite excuse, or is this a helpful guide to our understanding of the play?

actually find out which political party he belongs to. He is alarmed by Lord Illingworth's views (some of which are remarkably radical), and later dismisses them as 'tainted with foreign ideas' (Act I, p. 22). Aware that patriotism always goes down well, he harps repeatedly on 'the beauty of our English home-life', and in the presence of ladies he has some flattering opinions on the importance of women as 'the intellectual helpmeet of man' (Act I, p. 22).

Kelvil's views also suggest he is a Malthusian, that is he believes the poor should abstain from sex rather than having large families to support. His own behaviour, however, suggests that he is not exactly abstinent and that Mrs Kelvil is far from being treated as an intellectual equal: she has been sent to the seaside with their eight children while he enjoys himself at the house party. Lady Caroline repeatedly gets his name wrong and calls him 'Mr Kettle'. This may suggest that he is full of hot air, or it may be an **allusion** to the saying 'the pot shouldn't call the kettle black' – in other words he is as hypocritical and as little concerned with real political issues as any of the aristocrats whose views he has disparaged. When Lady Stutfield finally manages to converse with him alone, she emerges confused – they discuss 'Bimetallism, as well as I remember' (Act III, p. 74). Given that her flirtation technique involves lavishing attention on the speaker, this suggests Mr Kelvil can bore even the best listener into a stupor.

ARCHDEACON DAUBENY

We might expect the Archdeacon, Dr Daubeny, as the sole clergyman, to embody the authority of the Church to which Mrs Arbuthnot is devoted. In fact, he makes no statements about religion, sexual morality or social justice. Lady Hunstanton speaks of his work among the poor 'with the assistance of his curates' (Act I, p. 19) – which suggests that he leaves the hard work to someone else. Nor does he say anything that might upset the even tenor of the lives of the rich – the sermons from his 'nice pulpit' (Act III, p. 71) are admired because they are cosily predictable.

Wilde makes the Archdeacon the visible half of a double act, the other being the absent Mrs Daubeny. His conversation is almost exclusively about his wife's ailments, which become a running joke in the play as her image becomes ever more grotesque in our minds. She is too deaf to hear his sermons (Act II, p. 56) – by choice, perhaps? – has lost the ability to remember recent events (Act III, p. 74), and 'Lives entirely on jellies' (Act III, p. 78). The Archdeacon's life appears to be dominated by his wife: he leaves the company early, as 'Tuesday is always one of Mrs Daubeny's bad nights' (Act III, p. 78). The exact comic nature of Dr Daubeny's character depends on the actor. Should he play a henpecked husband submitting to what Lord Illingworth calls 'The tyranny of the weak over the strong' (Act III, p. 69)? Whatever the nature of their relationship, the invisible Mrs Daubeny is a wicked caricature of the Victorian feminine ideal: passive, silent, incapable of sensual pleasure and completely unaware of the world beyond her home.

LORD ALFRED

Lord Alfred's only distinguishing features are his debts and his gold-tipped cigarettes. He is selfish enough to ignore his creditors – 'they write; I don't' (Act I, p. 24) – and this perhaps offers some light on how the luxurious lifestyle of the other aristocrats is maintained. The role offers a young actor a chance to play an enjoyable caricature of a dim-witted lord; this has been a popular dramatic and literary stereotype since the seventeenth century. Here Alfred's function is to provide a contrast with the hard-working Gerald. Judging by their choice of slang – they both think of themselves as 'chaps' (Act I, p. 23) – they are about the same age. It is quite possible that he has been invited to provide Hester with a suitor the ladies consider more appropriate than a bank clerk, though the audience will be more likely to share her republican sentiments after seeing him.

LORD ILLINGWORTH

Wilde promised Sir Herbert Beerbohm Tree, the first to play the role, that Lord Illingworth would be something new to the English stage. 'He is certainly not natural. He is a figure of art,' Wilde told Tree. Illingworth's priorities are style, elegance and wit. He dominates the company from the moment he enters – mainly because he never makes a remark that is not capable of making them laugh, or think, or both. He is always expressing **paradoxical** ideas,

CONTEXT

Wilde was shortly to write his **comedy** *The Importance of Being Earnest* in which a character invents an imaginary invalid called Bunbury needing constant attention; he provides the perfect excuse to avoid unwanted appointments. Is the Archdeacon in actual fact a Bunburyist?

CONTEXT

The most entertaining instance of this popular stereotype is Bertie Wooster, created by P. G. Wodehouse (1881–1975). In novels such as *The Code of the Woosters* (1938) Bertie gets into regular scrapes with girls, money and difficult aunts but is always helped by his imperturbable manservant, Jeeves.

CONTEXT

Herbert Beerbohm Tree (1853–1917) was one of the most respected actor-managers of the day. He was known for character roles such as the sinister Svengali, which needed heavy make-up and eccentric mannerisms; in 1880 he played a caricature of Wilde in a play called *Where's the Cat?* He was also popular in the role of an aristocratic seducer preying on a virtuous girl, such as the Duke in Henry Arthur Jones' *The Dancing Girl* (1891). Wilde had some reservations about letting him play the role of Illingworth, afraid he would bring too strong a flavour of **melodrama**, although Tree's actual performance was praised for its 'artistic quietude'.

but he does so in a way that appears so easy that the audience almost have the sense that he is expressing their own thoughts (George Bernard Shaw once satirically complained in the *Saturday Review* that he was 'the only person in London who cannot sit down and write an Oscar Wilde play at will'). His comment 'The House of Commons really does very little harm', for example (Act I, p. 18), is not only a neat line to squash the tedious Mr Kelvil but offers such a memorable mental image of bumbling MPs that it ensures at least a temporary agreement.

Illingworth is quite clear that he does not always mean what he says: 'Taking sides is the beginning of sincerity, and earnestness follows shortly afterwards, and the human being becomes a bore' (Act I, p. 18). Most of the house party do not wish or expect him to be sincere; they wish him to entertain them, and he does so with the unselfconscious ease of a peacock displaying his tail. A large part of his attraction lies in suppressed energy: he never does anything physically taxing, but the speed and snap of some of his retorts – 'What are American dry goods?' asks Lady Hunstanton; Illingworth instantly replies, 'American novels' (p. 16) – make him seem like the most vividly alive person on the stage. While he dominates public conversation he does not, like the other men, assume that he has a right to monopolise a private conversation. He clearly takes pleasure in his witty exchanges with Mrs Allonby, and their mutual attraction seems at least partly based on their enjoyment of playing with words and ideas. They often seem to speak in a code, almost as if they were still performing to the rest of the company – although they are both too well mannered, it seems, to compete for attention when the party is assembled.

His carefully constructed witty public persona makes Lord Illingworth a mysterious figure. His replies are not merely clever; they are also quite impersonal. He talks about ideas, about America, about other people, about the sexes, but very little about his feelings, his tastes or his life. He tells Gerald: 'I like you so much' (Act I, p. 27), but his plan to kiss Hester is grounded in a desire to prove that 'I always succeed in whatever I try' (Act I, p. 29) rather than in any strong feelings. Consequently it comes as a shock when he confronts Mrs Arbuthnot and we learn that he has certainly been capable of powerful emotions in his youth. However, his exact feelings in the past, and, even more, his attitude to that past now, are decisions that the actor playing him must make and find a way to demonstrate.

On discovering Gerald's identity, Lord Illingworth tells Mrs Arbuthnot: 'my life seemed to be quite complete. It was not so. It lacked something, it lacked a son. I have found my son now, I am glad I have found him' (Act II, p. 58). Whether this is the beginning of love or whether Gerald is just a new accessory is not spelled out in the text – on stage it may be spoken very sincerely or treated as a passing thought. Afterwards, however, both parents become violently competitive and both try to win Gerald through underhand means. Illingworth admits that he has deliberately made Gerald 'discontented' in order to attract him to the job (Act II, p. 60). When he meets opposition, he tries a seductive display of self-assurance. He assures Gerald that 'The future belongs to the dandy' (Act III, p. 67) and describes the influence that can be exerted through personal style and charm.

However, this suggests that Illingworth has a more mercenary approach to his own elegance than is apparent at first. Rather than developing a witty persona to comment on the world, he exploits it to gain power in polite society. His battles of wit with Mrs Allonby suggest that he treats women as equals, but among men he expresses a misogynist attitude. He considers that women have a great deal of informal influence – hence 'One should always tell them' they are clever (Act III, p. 68) – but believes them to be manipulative and illogical. His persistence in trying to kiss Hester even while trying to win over Gerald suggests he takes for granted that women are really 'of no importance'. Perhaps he even wants to teach Gerald that very lesson. For all his radical sympathies, he cannot grasp that no means no.

Illingworth's class pride is also considerable. He boasts to Gerald of being one of the 'Harfords' (Act III, p. 70), and makes it rudely clear to Mrs Arbuthnot that marriage to her would be a sacrifice. His last act is to remind her of the class gap between her and 'people of one's own rank' (Act IV, p. 111). Wilde is sometimes accused of

CONTEXT

'American dry goods' signified many items including clothing and furniture. Dry-goods stores like Lord & Taylor in New York – founded in 1826 – were the forerunner of the big department store chains. Hester's father is part of a highly successful enterprise and most of the company would have shopped at a similar store in England. They just consider the owners to be beneath them.

CONTEXT

In his performance Herbert Beerbohm Tree was keen to stress through gesture and expression that Lord Illingworth had real affection for Gerald.

giving a complex play about relationships a **melodramatic** ending, but Illingworth has throughout valued and exulted in power – whether sexual, political or social – and he is consistent to himself. He has the intelligence to understand how power works; it gives him a contempt for some of his own class and also for the strategies they use to retain their power by preserving the 'slavery' of the poor (Act I, p. 18). However, he has no apparent inclination to follow up his political insights. In the end, despite the real affection he may have for Gerald, Lord Illingworth is not capable of a love that changes the character. His charm and brilliance give us a great deal of pleasure, but we also see that he wastes his talents and presents a threat to others.

MRS ARBUTHNOT

Mrs Arbuthnot lives a modest lifestyle in a secluded spot. She is a pillar of the local church and spends much of her time there. She does embroidery – possibly to beautify the church, or to eke out her living – and she cares for the sick and the poor. She is probably an active member of at least one philanthropic organisation, as Lady Hunstanton wonders whether she and Lord Illingworth might have a common interest in the 'Housing of the Poor' (Act II, p. 49). Lady Hunstanton takes pleasure in her company and thinks of her as a 'sweet saint' (Act IV, p. 90). Her religious nature makes itself apparent in her frequent quotations and **allusions** from the Bible, and she sometimes compares herself to biblical characters such as Hannah, the mother who longed for a child (Act IV, p. 98).

While Mrs Arbuthnot is undoubtedly sincere in her religion, she is also bitterly aware that it is a refuge rather than an inclination. She has, she tells her son, always felt real desire for 'the pleasant things of life' – including sunshine and company – but considers that she has 'no right' to them (Act IV, p. 99). When she does appear in company she is often discourteous, resolutely refusing any cue to frivolity as if she also denies herself the right to give pleasure. She feels herself completely defined by the act of giving herself to George Harford and bearing a child out of wedlock. She speaks to Gerald of the affair as if it happened to someone else: 'She was very young, and – and ignorant of what life really is' (Act III, p. 86). This is certainly true – it is clear that she was an innocent and passionate

girl in her 'father's garden' (Act II, p. 58), as Illingworth himself
admits. But she cannot manage to forgive herself; she accuses
Illingworth not just of neglect and betrayal but of the destruction
of her very nature: 'her life was ruined, and her soul ruined, and
all that was sweet, and good, and pure in her ruined also' (Act III,
p. 86).

Mrs Arbuthnot is in fact conforming, quite unconsciously, to the
way a 'ruined' woman was supposed to act according to all the
conventions of upper-class society, and to how such women were
usually portrayed in the drama of the time. It does not occur to her
to flout these conventions and think out her situation afresh. So she
behaves like a penitent in a novel: she denies herself despite the fact
she is not poor; she endorses all the harsh things that are said about
women in her situation; and while her secret appears to be safe, it
does not stop her mercilessly lashing herself with epithets such as
'leper' and 'lost soul' (Act III, p. 86). She agrees with Hester that
sinful women should be punished; she may not approve the priggish
insistence that the children should also suffer, but she bitterly
accepts that 'It is one of God's terrible laws' rather than trying to
argue her son's case with Hester (Act III, p. 81). She even dresses
to fit the part of a penitent in sombre black, although her choice of
'velvet' suggests that the sensuous side to her nature has not been
completely squashed.

His mother's self-imposed punishment has had its effect on Gerald;
he still lives with her in his twenties and she strongly resists the idea
of his leaving her, resorting to emotional blackmail, trying to make
him feel guilty that he has 'hurt' her in the past, even though the
same could be said of any child. It causes her anguish and confusion
that ultimately she loves him so much that she cannot repent of
what she did. Rather than seeing her child as a force to make her a
better person, she sees him as a kind of devil's bargain. Her sin is
'the price I paid for you – the price of soul and body' (Act IV,
p. 99). The intensity with which she clings to Gerald makes her a
rather unsympathetic figure. Her hatred of Illingworth has also
damaged her. She cannot, in the end, disentangle it from her love
for Gerald: 'I have two passions, Lord Illingworth: my love of him,
my hate of you. You cannot kill those. They feed each other'

? QUESTION

Examine Wilde's
use of Bible stories
and quotations in
*A Woman of No
Importance*. What
do they suggest
about the
characters?

(Act IV, p. 109). This corrosive aspect to her character combines with a passionate resistance to his class-bound assumptions that he can take his son simply because he is a Harford; this makes her more sympathetic to the audience.

Although Mrs Arbuthnot's situation was a common one on the Victorian stage, it is treated here with a rare honesty and originality. Wilde recognises the fact that conventions and literary stereotypes can shape reality as much as reflect it. Mrs Arbuthnot needs to find the imagination, as well as the charity, to forgive herself and others.

STRUCTURE

Unlike a novel or a poem, where the reader can move forward or back at will, a play is an experience in time. Victorian playwrights had a clear sense of how this experience should be organised to keep the audience alert and interested, constantly wondering what would happen next and expecting events to make sense in the light of what they had already learned. A **well-made play** begins with a clear **exposition** which spells out to the audience – preferably with subtlety so that it is barely noticeable – what they need to know before they can interpret the action. Wilde deals with this in such a leisurely fashion that the craftsmanship is almost undetectable. The focus seems to be on the relationships between the aristocrats, but he also sets up the tentative courtship of Hester and Gerald and makes it clear that money may be an obstacle. He ensures that we are very aware of the rules of aristocratic society on which their future depends. He creates **suspense**, firstly by Mrs Allonby's challenge to Illingworth to kiss 'the Puritan' (Act I, p. 31), and then by bringing down the curtain on the mystery about the 'woman of no importance' (Act I, p. 32).

The play goes on to the **development and complication** of the story and raises the level of tension in the audience as two stories unfold. Hester's puritanism is established as an obstacle to her love of Gerald; it is also shown to be a threat to Mrs Arbuthnot, who hears her pronouncing on the fate of the female sinner. As we learn of the old affair between Lord Illingworth and Mrs Arbuthnot we

CHECK THE BOOK

William Archer's *Play-Making* (1912) was an invaluable workshop manual for the aspiring Victorian playwright and explores the techniques used by the leading playwrights of his day. It lays out clearly the structure of a well-made play such as *A Woman of No Importance*. It is still possible to acquire a copy of this work; it has been reprinted as recently as 2006.

see a conflict developing between them; the emotions are so strong that Mrs Arbuthnot's decision to let Gerald go at the close of Act II cannot be decisive, and the audience looks forward to the next phase. The struggle continues to develop in Act III, and the past now breaks in on the present; as we see changes in Gerald's character we realise that not only his mother's happiness but Hester's is at stake. The situation becomes complex as the two women come together to try to change Gerald's mind. Now there is a new conflict, because the secret of his birth has the potential to drive them apart. Secrets are at the heart of the classic Victorian plot and this one becomes increasingly potent as everyone has a vital stake in it: inevitably, somebody will lose Gerald.

The play reaches its **crisis** just in time for the third act curtain, when the two strands of the story – the plot to kiss Hester and the parental struggle over Gerald – become entwined. This is traditionally the point in the well-made play when the spectators expect shocks and surprises and the curtain comes down on not less than two. The interval will see the audience eager to discover how the action will work itself out; while they may not guess what will happen, there will be a specific confrontation that they long to see – what French dramatists called a *scène à faire*. The scene everyone will anticipate most eagerly in Act IV is the next meeting between mother and son. Wilde does not disappoint. Parent and child confrontations have always been a vital ingredient of exciting drama. Many in the audience will be familiar with the one between mother and son in *Hamlet*. However, Wilde surprises us; while Gerald appears to have the moral high ground, speaking up for marriage, his mother passionately refuses and fights her corner. Hester then provides a stunning **reversal of expectations** by taking Mrs Arbuthnot's side, and on explicitly religious grounds. The audience will have hoped for this **denouement** from the outset, but Wilde has managed to make it seem impossible until this scene.

The play ends with a **resolution**. It is not enough that we know there will be a happy ending; there are loose ends to be tied. Some of these are a function of the plot: Lord Illingworth is discomfited – not simply as a seducer, but as an aristocrat faced with a newly independent bourgeois family. But the structure of the play is also

CONTEXT

Well-made plays were not uncommon during the first half of the twentieth century: J. B. Priestley's *An Inspector Calls* (1946), with its intertwined series of unexpected disclosures, climaxing in a final, dramatic revelation, could be described as a well-made play, as could Agatha Christie's *The Mousetrap* (1952).

CONTEXT

Shakespeare's *Hamlet* (c.1601) contains a scene in which Hamlet, the Prince of Denmark, stormily reproaches his widowed mother for marrying his uncle – the murderer of his father. A later and equally stormy confrontation occurs in Noël Coward's play of 1924, *The Vortex*. Here the son is outraged by his mother's younger boyfriend.

carefully finished in terms of language and **imagery**. Mrs Arbuthnot quotes Lord Illingworth's words about child-parent relationships back at him, and also unconsciously echoes his words at the close of Act I when she calls him 'A man of no importance' (Act IV, p. 112). She thus asserts her centrality in the play just as the young people come in from the garden – a location once associated with illicit love, but now with marriage – and place her at the centre of a new family.

LANGUAGE AND STYLE

Once you have read or seen a play by Oscar Wilde you can always recognise his style. Only Wilde characters speak in this distinctive way, working within a set of complex rules about both the matter and the manner of conversation. As far as the matter is concerned, they accurately reflect the rules of polite speech among the Victorian upper class. It was not proper to express strong emotions, neither was it proper to dominate a conversation, interrupt, or forget that speech was rationed: there was a tacit understanding that young people such as Hester would speak less than their elders and that women would speak less than men. It was also inappropriate to discuss certain subjects – such as money or sex – or to make disparaging remarks about people who, for all you knew, might be friends of those present. It was extremely improper to swear.

The continual breaking of these rules charges Wilde's dialogue with energy. The ordered conversational surface is frequently disturbed by flurries of passion. Hester, for instance, raises her voice for an unwanted political harangue, and her insult about Lord Henry Weston (Act II, p. 45) changes the mood by making the guests angry; they have to struggle visibly not to express this directly. Mrs Arbuthnot shatters a carefully established tone of civilised frivolity with a serious answer to a trivial question; when Lady Hunstanton suggests that women should 'forgive everything' (Act III, p. 76), she expects Mrs Arbuthnot to be as flippant as Lord Illingworth and Mrs Allonby when they speak of forgiving 'gigantic intellects' and 'adoration' (Act III, p. 75) – not raise a social problem. When the men are absent, the ladies' coffee-time conversation becomes risqué enough to shock the audience. Even Lord Illingworth swears in the last act, although Mrs Arbuthnot's timely blow with a glove renders the word inaudible. Other characters keep the rules, but manipulate them cleverly to make a point; the ladies know just how to use tact in order to punish Hester for her blunder about Lady Caroline's brother.

But if they struggle to keep to the rules about subject matter, characters have no trouble in obeying the rules about manner: everyone in a Wilde play is exceedingly articulate. Even in deep distress they obey the rules of grammar. Virtually every sentence has, as Victorian grammar books insisted, a subject, a verb and an object, and characters quite commonly engage in fancy sentence construction. When an unhappy and confused Gerald demands that his mother marry Illingworth, he speaks in a way he must have learned from the study of Latin oratory at school, piling phrase on phrase and repeating the key term: 'This marriage, this necessary marriage, this marriage that, for obvious reasons, must inevitably take place' (Act IV, p. 95). We always have the feeling that nobody begins a sentence without knowing exactly how it will end.

Wilde's dialogue has been called 'artificial', but it is not attempting to mimic real speech; rather, it springs from characters who have been constructed to enjoy their own artifice. Most of them take real pleasure in talk as an art form, as Wilde did himself. To speak his dialogue properly it is essential for the actor to control the breath and to maintain a posture that is both upright and relaxed in order to keep the flow of air constant; as a result, the characters themselves will have a studied grace of movement – they will look like actors, like people committed to entertaining an audience. The female characters demonstrate this through the assurance with which they facilitate the flow of conversation; all of them, especially the hostess, Lady Hunstanton, are constantly asking questions such as 'What have you been talking about?' or adding 'is it not?' to invite a reply. Both sexes are more than willing to let an accomplished speaker 'take the floor' and speak at length, showing by their responses that they are an appreciative audience. Mrs Allonby's long speech about the Ideal Man, for instance, is like an operatic aria, and it gets verbal applause from the characters – Lady Stutfield says: 'It has been quite, quite, entrancing' (Act II, p. 41).

 CHECK THE BOOK

Neil Sammells' *Wilde Style: The Plays and Prose of Oscar Wilde* (2000) considers the 'radicalism and modernity' of *A Woman of No Importance* and the way that the characters consciously deploy the styles of the literature of the period to organise their relationships.

It may prompt the audience to clap too. The best speakers are also the most playful; they encourage and compete with each other; they offer cues for a witty remark, such as Mrs Allonby's challenge: 'Define us as a sex' (Act I, p. 28). Lord Illingworth's reply – 'Sphinxes without secrets' – uses one of Wilde's chief comedic devices, that of **paradox**, a statement that apparently contradicts itself. While the structure of such a remark signals that it is to be taken as a joke, paradox often contains a sharp insight. Illingworth's remark that 'The youth of America is their oldest tradition' (Act I, p. 17), for example, deflates a political **cliché** and makes the audience look again at Anglo-American relationships in the play. The number of such remarks in the play not only adds to the fun; it also emphasises the paradoxical nature of the situations, such as the argument between mother and son in which she refuses to marry.

The general level of articulacy means that there is a fine line between conscious and unconscious wit. Lady Hunstanton, for instance, makes a number of comments which are funny because they create an incongruous image, such as her account of the death of Lord Illingworth's elder brother: 'he was killed in the hunting field. Or was it fishing, Caroline? I forget' (Act II, p. 51). Is this a sign of real confusion on her part, or is this a deliberately dotty style that permits her to get away with discreetly subversive statements such as her comment: 'no younger son has ever had such good luck' (Act II, p. 51)? Certainly Wilde and his characters ensure that nobody who is not amusing commands attention for very long. Mr Kelvil and Sir John, for example, are only allowed to talk freely offstage, and the comedy lies in the way the company manages to put a slightly risqué spin on the topics they have been spared: 'Bimetallism! Is that quite a nice subject?' (Act III, p. 74). When Lady Hunstanton says to Mrs Allonby, 'How clever you are, my dear! You never mean a single word you say' (Act II, p. 41), she is (probably) not being rude, but showing appreciation for the style with which Mrs Allonby delivers opinions; the speaker is not necessarily expected to mean them if they provide entertainment.

There are characters who do not subscribe to this code, such as Mrs Arbuthnot and Hester, who complains: 'You laugh at the simple and the pure' (Act II, p. 44). However, the play is not simply

CONTEXT

Bimetallism is the use of gold and silver as legal tender in a fixed ratio to each other – not a very lively topic for a potential seducer.

divided into the sincere and the artificial. Both of these women are extremely articulate. They know the rules about when to speak and when to be silent. They choose to flout them, and the effect on the company is as definite – if not as pleasant – as that of an Illingworth monologue. Their emotions are strong but they do not 'mean what they say' in the sense of expressing themselves in a literal way. Both of them use the language of the Bible constantly. In Hester's case the **allusions** chart a spiritual journey: at the beginning she uses, not very accurately, references to the Old Testament which describe a God of sternness and judgement, who punishes the children for 'the sins of the parents' (Act III, p. 80). At the end of the play, she is closer to the language of the New Testament with 'God's law is only Love' (Act IV, p. 102). The way that she remains within the language she has always used allows us to believe in her change of heart.

Mrs Arbuthnot's language draws on more varied sources. She uses a great deal of **hyperbole**. She knows Gerald was never left to die 'of hunger and of want' (Act II, p. 58). She is not confessing to drug addiction when she tells her son the story of his mother and claims 'no anodyne can give her sleep! no poppies forgetfulness!' (Act III, p. 86). She is not exaggerating because she is deluded, or even simply as a method of making others feel guilty. Rather, she is employing the kind of language that would be used in a moral tract or an appeal by a charity of the 'blankets and coals' kind – not the language of social outcasts themselves, but of the people who decide their fate. 'Fallen' women themselves were expected to be meek and silent, and she seems to have passed her secluded life being just that. Hence, when she does speak, the only language she can find is that of moral tracts and clichéd literature. It provides her with words of self-reproach and self-hate, such as 'tainted thing' (Act IV, p. 97) and 'leper' (Act III, p. 86). Despite this, she eventually manages to express her honest conviction that Gerald is 'more to me than innocence'. This is a radical statement, and it is not surprising that she asks him: 'don't you understand?' (Act IV, p. 99). It is a difficult idea for someone as conventional as Gerald to grasp. She is a worthy adversary to the witty Lord Illingworth, and the clash of their linguistic styles adds greatly to the energy of the play.

? QUESTION

Compare the distinctive use of language by two or more of the main characters. What does it tell you about them?

THEMES

INNOCENCE AND EXPERIENCE

Lord Illingworth says that 'The Book of Life begins with a man and a woman in a garden' (Act I, p. 31). Virtually all of Wilde's original audience would have known the Bible well enough to realise that this is an **allusion** to the story of Adam and Eve, who live in the Garden of Eden in a state of happiness and innocence until the serpent tempts Eve to eat the forbidden fruit and she persuades Adam to do the same. Now a sin has been committed, God expels them from Paradise and they are subject to pain and death. The story was understood to teach that mankind was inherently sinful and incapable of recovering that lost innocent happiness. It was also widely understood to mean that woman, the first sex to commit a sin, was inferior to man, and that part of her sinfulness was her ability to seduce him from the right path. This view of inherent sinfulness coexisted with an idea that had begun with the **Romantic** movement at the close of the eighteenth century: that children are born good and are damaged by the world around them. Consequently the Victorians tended to sentimentalise children and to equate a lack of knowledge with innocence itself. In particular, young girls were shielded from sexual knowledge, even those who were lucky enough to be allowed a reasonably broad education.

Throughout the play Wilde uses images of gardens and associates them with sexual temptation. We learn that George and Rachel began their affair in a garden (Act II, p. 58). It is in the garden that Lord Illingworth tries to kiss Hester (Act III, p. 87). Mrs Allonby flirts with him in the conservatory, an appropriately artificial version of a garden. Gerald and Hester go into the garden to discuss their marriage plans. They are the most 'innocent' characters. They are both very young and have seen very little of the world – Hester has been raised in the country and Gerald lives in a small town. However, their story is not told as a simple conflict between virtue and vice but rather as a painful process through which the innocent acquire a knowledge that allows them to function as mature adults. Gerald, popular with all the adults, lacks a sense of self. He has never questioned the assumption that 'No nice girl' (Act III, p. 86)

CONTEXT

Jean-Jacques Rousseau (1712–78) contended that humankind was good by nature and corrupted by society. He suggested that children should be brought up close to nature. His influence on the nineteenth-century image of the child as an innocent was visible in the writings of the English Romantic poets such as William Wordsworth (1770–1850).

can be seduced, because this fits his overall understanding of a world divided into 'good' and 'bad' people. Nonetheless, he has always relied on others to tell him which are which. He swings like a weathercock from Lord Illingworth's sophistication to the harsh and unforgiving views put forward by his mother and Hester. He learns that the world is more complex than this only when he is faced with a terrible **paradox**: his mother has brought him up in such innocence and ignorance because the strength of her love for him is rooted in his 'sinful' origins; she values him so much *because* she is not a 'nice girl' in his sense of the word.

While Gerald is 'tempted', in the sense that Lord Illingworth offers him an exciting life, Hester is not; she is so frightened of Illingworth's attempt to kiss her that she is in no danger of being seduced. Her 'innocence' is simply the ignorance of a carefully shielded young girl. What she has to learn is that some women can feel desire and that this does not put them beyond forgiveness. Her real 'temptation' is to self-righteousness, to demand punishment for others for sins she does not want to commit. Both Hester and Gerald could be considered 'sinful' in their original innocence, because they pass judgement on others without compassion or reflection. Both learn, and then commit acts conventionally perceived as 'sinful'. Hester actively encourages an unmarried mother to refuse to marry the father of her child, and even earns the label '*fin-de-siècle* person' from Lord Illingworth (Act IV, p. 110). Like Adam, Gerald takes the advice of Hester, the woman he loves, rather than a father figure. Both of them become better people for their loss of 'innocence', and perhaps we should see them as worthy of the 'garden' at the end of the play.

AMERICA

As the curtain rises on *A Woman of No Importance* the first thing we see is an English aristocrat out to make a young American uncomfortable. Lady Caroline's questions about 'country houses' in America (Act I, p. 6) are not requests for information but hints that Hester may not know how to behave at Hunstanton. Soon the clash of cultures is directly articulated. Lady Caroline remarks that in her youth she never met anyone who worked: 'It was not considered the thing' (Act I, p. 7). We might expect Hester's retort, 'In America

CONTEXT

In a skit – a short **satirical** piece of writing – on *A Woman of No Importance* in the June 1893 edition of *Theatre*, Hester introduces herself thus: 'I am an unconventional American. I have no accent and I despise the aristocracy; that is why I am staying with them. (*To Gerald*) Let us flirt.'

CHECK THE BOOK

For an account of the last days of American frontier life and a background to Wilde's more rugged American adventures, read David Lavender's *The Penguin Book of the American West* (1965), which contains many photographs of the period.

CONTEXT

Hester's social conscience is also related to her puritanism, the religion of America's Founding Fathers. There is an association in puritan ideology between the cheque and balance book and one's moral life – a sense of working hard to drive out sin. This puritan work ethic fits with Hester's (and America's) perception of English society as somehow ornamental, irresponsible and lacking sobriety.

those are the people we respect most' (Act I, p. 8), to leave Lady Caroline discomfited; but her reply, 'I have no doubt of it', suggests that the hard-working Gerald and Hester, the daughter of a self-made millionaire, are definitely 'not considered the thing'.

In the extended discussion about Americans that follows, several of Lord Illingworth's remarks – such as the comment about good Americans going to Paris when they die (Act I, p. 17) – would have been familiar to those who had read Wilde's bestseller *The Picture of Dorian Gray* (1891). Here they suggest an in-group enjoying the guilty pleasure of repeating a joke we might now call xenophobic. For these English aristocrats, Americans like Hester are nobodies. When the inevitable question 'Who are Miss Worsley's parents?' arises (Act I, p. 16), there is no answer that relates to peerages, noble families or country seats. Rather, it will be about work – 'not considered the thing'. They do not care to discuss how Hester's father makes his money: to talk about what was known as 'trade' was considered vulgar.

Hester has a point, then, when she complains they 'shut out from your society the gentle and the good' (Act II, p. 44). However, when she announces that 'In America we have no lower classes' (p. 43), the young millionairess is deluding herself. In 1890 the Superintendent of the Census had announced that the frontier, the land of opportunity anyone could take and tame with their own hands, no longer existed. The Federal government struggled to control companies fighting over major projects such as transport and irrigation, and there was widespread corruption – as Mr Kelvil smugly reminds the company. On both sides of the Atlantic the problem of poverty remained. Hester's image of English society as a 'leper in purple' (Act II, p. 44) ignoring its poor drew cheers in the US production, but the harsh weather of the late 1880s and the ruthless exploitation of minor landholders had led to terrible conditions for American farmers. Hester's idealism reflects the American Dream of a world where hard work is enough to achieve success. She announces: 'we are trying to build up something that will last longer than brick or stone' (Act II, p. 43) – but perhaps this is the millionaire's daughter speaking.

Hester may fairly claim that 'You are unjust to women in England' (Act II, p. 45); certainly the victims of Lady Caroline's brother would agree. However, her idea of 'justice' appears to involve equal punishment rather than equal rights – hardly an image of a new world. When, at the end, she takes Mrs Arbuthnot as her 'mother' and asks her to come and live abroad, it is of a new place altogether that she speaks, 'other countries over sea, better, wiser, and less unjust lands' (Act IV, p. 100). If this means America, it reflects her faith as much in her own social circles as in the American Dream itself. However, if the bored aristocrats despise the America they know (a little), they have nothing comparable to offer.

DANDYISM AND POWER

Lord Illingworth tells Gerald that 'The future belongs to the dandy' (Act III, p. 67). Wilde considered himself a **dandy**, frequently quoting from the French poet Baudelaire, who advocated artifice over nature, a commitment to personal style and originality, and a disdain for the common and the commercial. Dandyism did not commit itself to a belief system; rather, it asserted that life was meaningless but that this was not particularly important; what mattered was to weather it with style. In England dandyism was personified in the early nineteenth century by Beau Brummell, the man who despite his own lowly origins established the style for male elegance based on simple, plain and expensive tailoring that was still the norm for Wilde's own era. Lord Illingworth's assertion that 'A well-tied tie is the first serious step in life' (Act III, p. 67) might almost be a quotation from Brummell.

Wilde's own style reflected the class mobility of Brummell rather than the snobbishness of Baudelaire. Dandyism was something that could be learned, like good taste or an appreciation of art; his brand of socialism was dedicated to making it possible for everyone to construct their own personality and to have a sense of self-worth and individuality – even if this meant challenging received ideas about politics, art or sexuality. While Baudelaire's idea of the dandy was misogynist, for Wilde a dandy could be male or female; the dandified hero of *An Ideal Husband* says that in London 'The men are all dowdies and the women are all dandies' (Act I, *Complete*

CONTEXT

The phrase 'American Dream' was coined in 1931 in John Truslow Adams' book *The Epic of America* to describe the difference in attitude between the Old and the New Worlds. It reflects the idea of America as a place where the availability of land and the opportunities for industrialisation made it possible for an individual to achieve spectacular financial success.

CONTEXT

Charles Baudelaire (1821–67) was one of France's most influential poets. In 1857 he produced his most famous volume of poems, *Les Fleurs du mal*. Their themes of sex and death were considered scandalous, and Baudelaire and his publishers were prosecuted.

CONTEXT

Beau Brummell (1778–1840) was the arbiter of fashion of the Regency period and made the suit and necktie the usual dress of the elegant man. He met the Prince Regent in 1793 and rapidly advanced in society, but overreached himself in 1813 when he remarked to the man standing next to the prince, 'Who's your fat friend?' The podgy prince never forgave him, and Brummell died in poverty.

CHECK THE BOOK

Ellen Moers' *The Dandy: Brummell to Beerbohm* (1978) provides a history of the dandy across the nineteenth century in England and France.

Works, p. 524). Mrs Allonby has the artifice and the playfulness of a female **dandy** in her bouts of wit with Lord Illingworth.

For both Illingworth and Mrs Allonby, their insouciance involves a lack of concern for others. This comes to the fore in their wager over Hester. For Mrs Allonby, it is partly motivated by jealousy of Hester's youth. It reminds us that the dandy's stance requires effort to maintain as one gets older, like a swan paddling furiously as it appears to glide over the water. Mrs Allonby may be feeling tired and resentful. For Illingworth, the wager is partly about sexual curiosity. However, it also springs from a conscious opposition to puritanism; he wants to break it down and put in its place the enjoyment of artifice and the pursuit of pleasure. Almost invariably, he refers to Hester as 'the Puritan', as if she represents a whole species rather than an individual. This may be why he does not play fair. He does not 'convert' or convince Hester – in fact, we never see him try. His attempt to kiss her does not seem to have been particularly subtle, and at no point in the play does she warm to him. He attacks rather than seeks to charm.

Wilde's focus on the relationship between dandyism and power is underlined by Illingworth's lecture to Gerald. This also indicates that Illingworth sees his own stylishness as a source of political influence, a way of getting 'women on your side' (Act III, p. 68). Such mercenary motives undercut the true dandy's cool detachment; Illingworth delights the audience on and offstage with his wit, but his dandyism lacks the essential component of delight in itself for its own sake.

This is not always the case with Wilde's dandies: for him dandyism is morally neutral. To be cool and witty in a Wilde play is not automatically a sign of decadence and selfishness; nor, as it often is in the **comedy of manners,** is wit the guarantee of goodness and common sense. Wilde's Lord Goring and the witty Mabel Chiltern in *An Ideal Husband* are the sanest and most charitable characters in the play. In *The Importance of Being Earnest* dandyism is the rule rather than the exception, and the plot is too absurd for morality to enter into the story. In *The Picture of Dorian Gray* a corrupt and dangerous dandy sets the whole **tragedy** in motion – however, he does not do so in the name of dandyism itself. Lord Illingworth is Wilde's only character who deliberately sets the dandy-puritan conflict in motion – and we are invited to ask ourselves, perhaps, whether he deserves the title of dandy. Wilde always keeps us guessing as to the ethical standing of his dandies; what we can always rely on is the wit with which these dandies enliven the story.

FAMILY

When Gerald learns his mother's past he is at a total loss how to sign a letter, feeling he has 'no right to any name' (Act IV, p. 93). For him family is closely bound up with identity, and this is true for the society into which Lady Hunstanton has invited him. Inheritance is one of the favourite topics of conversation. Lord Illingworth's pedigree is complicated. It has to be, of course, so that Mrs Arbuthnot does not know exactly who has offered her son a position; but as Lady Caroline, the human encyclopaedia of the peerage, explains how he inherited his title, Wilde makes a telling point about the priorities of this society:

> There was poor Margaret's baby. You remember how anxious she was to have a boy, and it was a boy, but it died, and her husband died shortly afterwards, and she married almost immediately one of Lord Ascot's sons, who, I am told, beats her.
>
> (Act II, p. 50)

The only point of interest here for Lady Caroline is Illingworth's lineage. She glosses over a history of unhappiness illuminated by Lady Hunstanton as she recalls Illingworth's parents. His estrangement from his father is also discussed in terms of its financial consequences. Lord Illingworth takes great pride in his family name and its presence in 'the Peerage' – even though he calls this book of English family trees 'the best thing in fiction the English have ever done' (Act III, p. 71). 'Fiction' might refer to the idea that not all heirs are in fact their fathers' sons. Or it might be an **allusion** to the purchase of honours, anathema to older families.

Though the word 'home' occurs several times in the play – Mr Kelvil praises 'home-life' (Act I, p. 22) and Mrs Allonby contemptuously calls Mrs Arbuthnot's house a 'happy English

CONTEXT

The comedy of manners generally focuses on the love intrigues of men and women in the middle and upper classes, and puts much emphasis on wit, elegance and sophistication. Restoration comedy is one of the finest examples of this genre, while Shakespeare's *Love's Labour's Lost* (1595) and *Much Ado About Nothing* (c.1598–9) can also be considered comedies of manners.

 QUESTION

Hester says: 'your English society seems to me shallow, selfish, foolish' (Act II, p. 44). To what extent is this a valid description of the world shown in the play?

...tinued

CHECK THE BOOK

Oscar Wilde: The Critical Heritage, edited by Karl Beckson (1970), is a compendium of critical responses to Wilde's work from 1881 onwards. It usefully charts the way that different eras have responded to the man and how this has affected judgements on his work.

CHECK THE BOOK

Russell Jackson's *Victorian Theatre: The Theatre in Its Time* (1989) contains a variety of source material dealing with all aspects of the drama of the period. It contains several contemporary essays on censorship and its effects.

home' (Act IV, p. 89) – the families we see are broken or incomplete. Mr Kelvil has sent his to the seaside, the older characters do not discuss their children, and Hester is an orphan. The only 'family' we see on the stage as a group is the highly combustible mix of Lord Illingworth, Mrs Arbuthnot and Gerald – but this is not so much a group as a tug of love over a child old enough to be independent. Both Illingworth and Mrs Arbuthnot have a clear idea what they stand to gain as an active parent: the company of Gerald. For Mrs Arbuthnot, this involves keeping her son to herself in a world with very narrow horizons. She uses the word 'child' a good deal, and her possessiveness already seems to have infantilised Gerald. For Illingworth, it involves treating Gerald as he would treat any young man to whom he has taken a fancy; the fact that they are father and son is a bonus, not to mention a convenient way of asserting rights over him. It does not, perhaps, involve his taking any responsibility. He implies, for instance, that he expects Gerald to drop Hester: 'she doesn't count' (Act IV, p. 105). The smooth assumption that he and Mrs Arbuthnot can have Gerald for six months apiece suggests that he sees his son as an object to be divided. An episode in the play conspicuous by its absence is a scene in which Gerald sees both parents together and makes a clear and rational statement of his feelings to them both.

Nevertheless, the play does close with an image of 'family'. There is a breadwinner, Hester; Gerald as both husband and son; and the woman they both call mother. All three have made deliberate choices about these roles, out of love rather than social convention. If this is an unorthodox grouping in terms of Mr Kelvil's domestic ideal, it is one that may work and find a future.

STAGING

Wilde's plays were all written to be staged in a theatre with a **proscenium arch** – a stage shaped like a box with one side removed. When the set depicts a room, the audience is like a fly on an invisible wall, watching characters who appear to carry on their lives oblivious of its presence. Everything on the stage is constructed to give the illusion of real life.

At first glance, then, the set would look ordinary. Wilde's original well-to-do audience would have seen rooms resembling their own and objects on the stage like those they possessed themselves. However, the play invests both the sets and the objects within them with considerable significance and asks us to read the apparently ordinary world carefully for clues about the characters and situations. The shift in setting from Hunstanton to Mrs Arbuthnot's house, for example, is a key moment in the play and reflects a shift in the balance of power between the aristocracy and the less well off. Lady Caroline in Act I turns mufflers and overshoes into weapons to ensure Sir John's constant attention. Letters lie about on tables ignored by the characters; but the nineteenth-century audience would have known that a letter could force the action into entirely new directions and would have kept a watchful eye on them. The sight of Mrs Arbuthnot's handwriting startles Lord Illingworth, and the audience will at once wonder why. Later the two of them will fight over his right to read a letter we have seen Gerald struggle to compose. In Act IV Mrs Arbuthnot's room is examined by Mrs Allonby and Lady Hunstanton with the thoroughness of police at a crime scene, and their conclusions about pictures and flowers are shared with us. Wilde is sometimes less specific about how **props** are to be used, but gives them to the actors as a tool for expressing their characters. For instance, the way Gerald smokes the cigarette given him in Act III by Lord Illingworth might indicate that he is not used to it – perhaps even that he has never been allowed to smoke. Lady Caroline's request for cotton after Hester's political speech (Act II, p. 46) indicates that she is sewing, something the actress might exploit in order to punctuate her own speeches with jabs of the needle.

Characters dressed in the same kinds of clothing as their nineteenth-century audience – although perhaps more expensively than most. But the clothes on stage would also convey a great deal of information about their income: Gerald's clothing would be less well cut than the clothes of the other men, for instance. Mrs Arbuthnot's black dress would stand out among the pretty evening dresses – and make it clear that that is exactly, consciously or not, what she wants.

CHECK THE BOOK

Neil Bartlett's *Who Was That Man? A Present for Mr Oscar Wilde* (1988) offers a critique of Wilde and includes an imaginary conversation with him.

CONTEXT

The actress Athene Seyler (1889–1990) commented that in nineteenth-century dresses a woman needs to 'swim' rather than walk.

CONTEXT

Max Beerbohm
was the younger
half-brother of
Herbert Beerbohm
Tree. He was the
drama critic for
the *Saturday
Review* and wrote
the cult novel
Zuleika Dobson
(1912). He was
renowned for
his cartoons and
witty **parodies**
of contemporary
writers such as
Henry James and
George Meredith.

CONTEXT

Watteau
specialised in
paintings of the
French aristocracy
at play. He
excelled in
showing the effect
of light on silk and
frequently painted
scenes from
theatrical
performances.

 **CHECK
THE NET**

Use the alphabetical
index at **www.
abcgallery.com** to
see some examples
of Watteau's
paintings online.

Wilde has made some definite assumptions about the performance style of the play. It is set in a world that expresses privilege. The actors need to express this sense of being at ease there. All well educated, the characters are able to negotiate their way through long and complex speeches; this will involve an upright posture. All of them – consciously or not – 'perform' for the company as they deliver **epigrams**, religious sentiments or political speeches, and so they will speak with the energy and clarity that this demands. Their clothing is formal, and in the case of the women it will demand balanced and graceful movement. These are consistently necessary to the successful performance of the play, but it is possible to stress different aspects of it at different points in time.

THE FIRST PRODUCTION

The poster for the original 1893 production showed the silhouette of a well-dressed woman in a melancholy attitude against a background of brilliant scarlet. The lettering looked like a private letter, hastily dashed off by an educated hand. It promised London society a staple treat – a play about a 'scarlet' woman with a secret. The Theatre Royal, Haymarket, was the grandest theatre of the 1890s, attracting the smart, the wealthy and the influential. Evening dress was compulsory. Max Beerbohm (1872–1956) noted in the *Saturday Review* that the audience was full of well-known people from 'the arts, literature, law and politics'. In short, it was like looking into a mirror. *A Woman of No Importance* showed society to itself. Sir Herbert Beerbohm Tree, who managed the theatre, directed the production and played Lord Illingworth, was careful to see that it did so. The silk and satin dresses were as luxurious as those of the audience; Mrs Allonby's gown of pink satin covered with pink roses and lined with black was perhaps the most dazzling. The design was based on the paintings of Jean Antoine Watteau (1684–1721), who showed aristocratic ladies playing at shepherdesses.

Tree softened some of the more subversive and original elements of the play. He insisted that Wilde cut a long speech by Lord Illingworth against puritan ideals in order to make the character more sympathetic. He made the most of the third act's **strong curtain** by having Mrs Arbuthnot swoon onto a couch rather than allow the moment of recovery and regrouping that Wilde's stage directions called for. However, he also cast Mrs Bernard Beere as Mrs Arbuthnot. She had once hoped to produce Wilde's political tragedy *Vera*, and brought an articulate authority to the role. Critics admired her 'Magdalen-red' hair – Mary Magdalen was the repentant prostitute who washed Jesus' feet with her tears; this implies that she understood the self-dramatising nature of the character as well as her intelligence. Tree cast his own wife, Maud Tree, as Mrs Allonby; this allowed them a great deal of licence in their flirtatious scenes, as the public did not feel too disturbed by them. He also cast a pair soon to be engaged as the lovers – Julia Neilson as Hester and Fred Terry as Gerald. Terry was a little too old for the role, but he was also popular in swashbuckling parts, modifying Gerald's dullness. Interestingly, Julia Neilson wore a dress of such expense that it seemed to undermine some of her sermons, perhaps a deliberate choice on Tree's part. If it all felt like an exclusive party hosted by Wilde rather than barbed social comment, there were still people in the audience who recognised their own codes and situations and took the chance to reflect on them. The play ran for one hundred and thirteen performances (to count as truly successful it needed three or four hundred).

LATER VERSIONS

A Woman of No Importance remains the least frequently revived of Wilde's comedies. For some time after the scandal, the only theatre willing to keep it in the repertory was J. T Grein's Independent Theatre. Grein admired Wilde and considered that he was in the tradition of Henrik Ibsen and George Bernard Shaw. There were only a few London revivals – 1907, 1953 and 1968 – and unlike the other Wilde comedies it has never been filmed. However, a production by Philip Prowse in 1991 made some radical innovations which stressed the way all Wilde's characters constructed selves through the use of wit and artifice. It broke down the distinction between art and nature. As the audience took their seats, they saw Lord Alfred playing croquet in bare feet on a lawn with a lily pond and ornamental urns. The opening dialogue took place in front of an enormous eighteenth-century landscape painting in a gilt frame. In the next act the lily pond was transformed into a circular sofa in clashing fabrics and the painting was replaced by a gold 'curtain'

CONTEXT

One of the most famous images of Mary Magdalen was painted by Titian c.1535: eyes raised piously to heaven, dressed in nothing but clouds of rich auburn curls. The Pre-Raphaelite school of painting active in the mid-Victorian period favoured red-headed models, and many of Wilde's audience would have been familiar with William Holman Hunt's painting *The Awakening Conscience* (1853). This depicts a young woman rising with an expression of stricken guilt from the lap of her seducer, auburn hair cascading down her back. Mrs Beere's hairstyle would certainly have suggested penitence, but it would also have had erotic overtones.

clearly made of wood. In the last act, the landscape painting could be seen forming the view through the windows of Mrs Arbuthnot's sitting-room, a plainly furnished space with curtains of midnight blue. The effect was to undermine any simplistic contrasts between 'real' and 'artificial' or 'country' and 'city', and show people continually engaged in the task of shaping themselves, like works of art, using language, clothing and setting. Hester's American 'outsider' status was underlined by using a black actress; it stressed that the process of building a self was taking place during a time of massive social upheavals across the world. The revival was a tribute to the radical originality of Wilde and stressed that the play is still alive with new theatrical possibilities.

THE TWENTY-FIRST CENTURY

CHECK THE NET

To view Max Beerbohm's famous sketch of Oscar Wilde, go to the National Portrait Gallery – **www.npg.org.uk** – and type Beerbohm into the artist search box.

In 2002 Peter Hall staged the play in more conventional style following his successful revival of *Lady Windermere's Fan*. The emphasis was on the social **satire**, and he treated it as a much darker play than its predecessor. Since then there have been several revivals at regional theatres – Ben Twist's production for the Pitlochry Festival in 2006 and Lucy Pitman-Wallace's for Salisbury Playhouse, for example. While the world Wilde knew is very different in the twenty-first century, actors can find much to convey to a modern audience in his careful documentation of the way people deploy their personal power over one another, whether it comes from experience, sexual magnetism or emotional blackmail; and as the relationship between Britain and the USA continues to change and develop, Lord Illingworth and Hester offer some interesting insights.

PART FOUR

CRITICAL HISTORY

ORIGINAL RECEPTION AND EARLY CRITICAL VIEWS

The first responses to *A Woman of No Importance* were mixed. Most people found something to admire, and most people also found elements they thought had spoiled the play. However, nobody seemed to agree as to which bits were which, mainly because they could not decide what kind of play it was. Was it a serious play about social issues ruined by frothy comedy such as the first act in the garden? Or was it a sophisticated society play which tipped into **melodrama** as Gerald discovers his paternity? One of the most thoughtful reviews, praised by Wilde for its 'luminous' quality, was by William Archer. Like several others, he described the witty comedic element as a serious flaw, evidence that Wilde was failing to take himself seriously; like others he also complained of the unattractive nature of the 'good' characters. Archer considered that the emotional outbursts from Mrs Arbuthnot were 'conventional'. While some suggested that this was because Wilde could not create good characters, Archer saw it as an attempt to win cheap popularity with sanctimonious sentiment. It did not occur to anyone to suggest that good characters do not necessarily have to be attractive ones and that the language of the popular theatre may be natural to them. Nevertheless, Archer considered that the play was 'on the very highest plane of modern English drama'. In fact, he said that it stood 'alone' – a statement he retracted when Pinero's *The Second Mrs Tanqueray* appeared that same year. What he admired was the restrained and compassionate treatment of 'fallen' women in both plays. Nonetheless, Wilde's more original mix of styles caused him difficulties.

Several critics of both the London and New York productions perceived the play as an attempt to imitate Ibsen's social-issue dramas. The *Era* commented on Hester's 'advanced' views. At this point, comparisons with Ibsen were usually meant to be pejorative and implied that the subject matter was not suitable for the stage.

> **CONTEXT**
>
> Archer (1856–1924) was one of the most influential theatre critics of his day, and a prolific translator. He was responsible for introducing English audiences to Ibsen with his translations of *Pillars of Society* (1880) and *A Doll's House* (1889). He produced a number of books, including *Masks or Faces?* (1888) about the psychology of acting and collaborated briefly with Shaw on *Widowers' Houses* (1892). Archer's review of *A Woman of No Importance* first appeared in April 1893 in the *World* and was reprinted in the *Theatrical World* for 1893. He also wrote a defence of this review in the *St James's Gazette* in June that year, again reprinted.

CONTEXT

Sir Arthur Pinero (1855–1934), author of some fifty plays, gave up a career in law to become an actor in 1874. His first play, *Two Hundred a Year*, was performed in 1877, and he wrote a series of successful **comedies**. It is for his social dramas that he is best remembered, however, notably *The Second Mrs Tanqueray* (1893), which made him arguably the most successful dramatist of his day.

One paper, for example, complained of the **naturalism** of the confidential talk between Gerald and Illingworth, considering that it verged on the shocking – 'the smoking-room is the proper theatre for such displays'. And although it enjoyed Hester's anti-British rants, the *New York Times* felt that Wilde's mind 'seems to be as impure as the River Thames by London Bridge'.

CRITICAL HISTORY

After his trials and imprisonment for homosexuality in 1895, the scandal attached to Wilde's name became entwined with his critical reputation. Contemporaries who outlived him saw his fate as tragic but dwelt on the surface brilliance of the plays, which they linked to a flaw in his psychology. Shortly after the First World War, for example, the novelist George Moore described his plays as 'superficial' and Wilde as 'third or fourth class'. This view of Wilde as a crowd pleaser who compromised his talent prevailed into the twentieth century. In 1967, for instance, John Russell Taylor was still proclaiming in *The Rise and Fall of the Well Made Play* (1967) that the attraction of his work lay in an 'element of barefaced charlatanism'. Nobody denied that the plays worked well in the theatre, but nobody was prepared to credit Wilde with more than a knack for light entertainment. Christopher S. Nassaar's *Into the Demon Universe: A Literary Exploration of Oscar Wilde* (1974) was one of the first books to take Wilde seriously. His analysis of *A Woman of No Importance* suggests that Mrs Arbuthnot's possessiveness is grounded in subconscious incestuous impulses – a contentious view, but one which at least encouraged others to look more closely at Wilde's work.

The last thirty years or so have seen a considerable number of critical works on Wilde which pay tribute to the originality of his thought and the breadth of his talent. Katharine Worth's *Oscar Wilde* (1983) places Wilde alongside pioneers of **subtext** such as Chekhov for his 'experiment in style' in the long and apparently aimless chat that reveals so much in Act I, suggesting that *A Woman of No Importance* is one of his most significant works. Kerry Powell documents Wilde's borrowings from European drama in *Oscar*

Wilde and the Theatre of the 1890s (1990), while Sos Eltis in *Revising Wilde: Society and Subversion in the Plays of Oscar Wilde* (1996) suggests that it is precisely the way he subverted these conventional plays about 'fallen women' in depicting the passionate and difficult Mrs Arbuthnot that makes *A Woman of No Importance* so powerful.

In the broader field of Wilde criticism his significance as a gay icon has been widely debated. Alan Sinfield's controversial *The Wilde Century: Effeminacy, Oscar Wilde and the Queer Moment* (1994) suggests that Wilde's own scandal was a catalyst for the establishment of a gay stereotype and that he had an ambivalent significance for gay men: 'As well as our Christ … Wilde was our Judas.' Wilde's Irish identity has also been reassessed after being virtually ignored for decades, most notably in Declan Kiberd's *Inventing Ireland: The Literature of the Modern Nation* (1995), which presents him as a 'militant republican'. Regenia Gagnier's collection *Critical Essays on Oscar Wilde* (1992) explores many different aspects of Wilde's life and works. Above all, it celebrates him in a role that covers his many identities and suggests that he is still a man of some importance: 'Wilde means many things to our time. Most important among them, he means … freedom and toleration.'

CONTEMPORARY APPROACHES

SIGNS AND SEMIOTICS

Semiotics is the study of signs. The discipline began with the work of the Swiss linguist Ferdinand de Saussure (1857–1913), who explained language as a system of words which have no *intrinsic* relationship to the things they signify but have meanings agreed upon by those who use them, and which distinguish them from other words for other things (for example, we know that in English 'cat' means a small furry animal and that 'cot' means something different). It was developed through writers such as Claude Lévi-Strauss (b.1908) and Roland Barthes (1915–80) to analyse all the varieties of sign systems that people use to convey meaning, such as gestures, clothing, decorations, food and manners. Because they

 CHECK THE BOOK
Martin Esslin's *The Field of Drama: How the Signs of Drama Create Meaning on Stage and Screen* (1987) is a very useful introduction to theatre semiotics which provides plenty of examples of sign systems at work in well-known plays.

of a sign given particular meaning by its context is provided by Robert Ross, Wilde's friend and former lover, who made a routine matter of etiquette into an act of kindness and defiance. On 25 September 1895 Wilde was briefly let out of prison to endure bankruptcy proceedings. Ross waited for hours in the corridor of the court, so that when Wilde was led by in handcuffs he could raise his hat to him and thus indicate that to him Wilde was a gentleman worthy of respect, not a criminal.

are arbitrary, the relationship between the **signifier** (the word or image or action) and the **signified** (the meaning conventionally ascribed to it) can change or slip.

This can be a helpful way to understand a piece of theatre, which is a formal arrangement of different kinds of signs. Take, for example, the use of names as they are spoken on the stage. At the simplest level we know that 'Mrs Arbuthnot' signifies a particular character. At another level, we know that the use of her surname in company also signifies that she is accepted by the rest of the house party as an equal in a way that 'Francis' the footman is not. Its meaning changes for us even more when Lord Illingworth enquires, 'why Arbuthnot, Rachel?' and she replies, 'One name is as good as another, when one has no right to any name' (Act II, p. 57). This adds several new layers of meaning. For example, it suggests she feels she has betrayed her own family; she could use her father's name, but chooses not to. She does *not* choose a name that might signify a member of the working class to a Victorian audience: it is hard to imagine that line being said about the name 'Bloggs', for instance. Gerald has quite complex feelings about his own surname and, like his mother, feels that there is a question of 'rights' involved. It could also be worth exploring the way that Mrs Arbuthnot and Lord Illingworth use the names 'George' and 'Rachel' when they are alone together. Conventionally, use of a first name signified a close relationship; but at different times in their dialogue it comes to signify affection, an attempt to get close in order to persuade, and even an expression of contempt.

Wilde uses clothing in similar ways. The text mentions Hester's expensive clothing from Paris; when she castigates the company for 'Living, as you all do, on others and by them' (Act II, p. 44), there is a tension between her dress as signifier of 'rich young woman' and the views that she expresses, which may make the audience ponder the complexity of her character. There is also an interesting slip between Lord Illingworth's last sight of Hester at the end of Act III – when she would certainly be wearing an evening dress in the latest style – and his scornful description of her as 'the Puritan in white muslin' (Act IV, p. 105). This sophisticated man glibly labels people rather than seeing what they are really like.

Gesture, too, carries a weight of significance – for instance the ways Lord Illingworth's gloves are handled in Act IV. When he removes them, it signifies the automatic politeness of his class – a gentleman would always remove his gloves in a private house – and Wilde does not bother to indicate when he does so. However, at the end, when he begins to put the gloves on, it may signify the final hardening of hostility by showing he does not intend to shake hands with Mrs Arbuthnot – a gentleman would never do so wearing gloves. When she picks up one of the gloves and strikes him, the gesture straightforwardly signifies anger; but it also carries a further meaning: to strike someone in the face with a glove meant that you were challenging them to a duel. Though not literally the case, the gesture carries associations of heroism which add to the stature of Mrs Arbuthnot. Similarly, when Lord Illingworth fails to pick up the glove – conveniently leaving it so that Gerald can read it yet another way, as a sign his mother has had a visitor – it signifies his haste to be gone; but associations with duelling also suggest themselves: failure to take up the glove after the blow signified cowardice or surrender. Throughout the play, the most trivial objects and idly spoken words carry multiple layers of meaning.

GENDERED CRITICISM

Thanks to *The Importance of Being Earnest*, Wilde is one of the most famous playwrights in the English-speaking world. Thanks to his trials and *De Profundis*, he is also one of the most famous homosexuals. Some versions of queer theory see a homoerotic **subtext** in several of his society dramas, linked particularly to the repeated theme of a relationship between an older and a younger man. Wilde's novel *The Picture of Dorian Gray* (1891) was explicit in its portrayal of a decadent aristocrat corrupting a beautiful youth, and some of the observations about women, society and personal appearance made by Lord Illingworth here are actually taken from the novel. This has encouraged some critics to suggest that this is Wilde's way of encoding the story of Illingworth's relationship with Gerald as one of male-male seduction, something that the censor would never have permitted to be overtly staged. The critic Lytton Strachey (1880–1932) suggested this as early as 1907. However, while this opens up interesting possibilities that most of the Victorian audience would have missed, it is also a rather reductive

> **CONTEXT**
>
> Lord Illingworth's comment to Gerald that 'women represent the triumph of matter over mind – just as men represent the triumph of mind over morals' (Act III, pp. 68–9) repeats word for word Lord Henry's speech in Chapter 4 of *The Picture of Dorian Gray* (*Complete Works*, p. 47), and is just one of a number of phrases and ideas also found in Wilde's novel.

> **CONTEXT**
>
> Queer theory is a strand of cultural theory which challenges society's ideas about gender and sexuality as fixed and immovable. It argues that our identities are shifting and ambiguous and that different meanings can coexist in the same text.

Gendered criticism continued

CHECK THE BOOK

The Picture of Dorian Gray can be found in Merlin Holland's *Complete Works of Oscar Wilde* (1994).

CHECK THE BOOK

Judith Butler's *Gender Trouble: Feminism and the Subversion of Identity* (1990) is a difficult but rewarding study of how people perform their gender.

reading of the complexity of the central relationships. Both parents, fighting over their son, use all the psychological weapons they can muster, and sexual magnetism is as useful to Illingworth as money and influence. While he uses many of the best lines originally given to the sinister Lord Henry Wotton in *The Picture of Dorian Gray*, this may simply be thrifty recycling on Wilde's part – or it may even be a way of indicating that Illingworth's charm is fake and unoriginal.

However, both queer and feminist criticism offer a further way of reading the behaviour of the characters. Judith Butler has suggested that gender itself is performative – that our gender (as opposed to our biological sex) is not innate. Rather, it is a role that we act out according to certain conventions which society has unconsciously decided are 'natural' for men and women. These conventions can be defied by individuals and are constantly in a state of flux as society adapts its expectations of gender to fit a changing world. The Victorians considered men and women to have marked 'natural' differences. This emphasis on difference would have been very visible in the play in terms of costume. Clothing reflected current ideal body images and these were in sharp contrast: the ideal woman was dainty, curvy and had a tiny waist, while the man was endowed with strong broad shoulders. The name of Mrs Allonby's husband, Ernest, means 'hairy' and reflects the Victorian tendency for men to sport beards, moustaches or whiskers. Male dress of the period was practical and plain, reflecting the idea of a working breadwinner; wealthy women wore tight corsets, frills and elaborately constructed dresses, difficult to move in, which showed that their husbands or fathers could keep them in idleness and underlined their dependency on men.

In *A Woman of No Importance* some characters struggle to maintain conventionally gendered positions, and this may lead the audience to question those conventions. Mrs Arbuthnot fulfils many Victorian expectations of motherhood – self-sacrifice, love for her child – but she is unmarried and unrepentant. Gerald is 'masculine' in asserting his freedom from maternal control, but his weepy dependence as the women decide his fate at the end of the play suggests he has difficulty in projecting the image of strength demanded of men. Mrs Allonby, on the other hand, is playfully acting out Victorian definitions of femininity. She knows that women are considered 'naturally' modest, with a natural reflex of blushing when their modesty is offended. But she is aware that this is not a 'natural' reaction but convention, and uses it for her own entertainment. She tells Lady Hunstanton: 'I like blushing' (Act IV, p. 90), showing how easily a gender role society considers to be set in stone can be manipulated.

QUESTION

To what extent could Wilde's characters be said to be 'performing' their gender or class?

PART FIVE

BACKGROUND

CHECK THE BOOK

Richard Ellmann's *Oscar Wilde* (1987) is a vivid, detailed and absorbing biography that uses much previously unpublished material made available by Wilde's grandson, Merlin Holland.

CHECK THE BOOK

Terry Eagleton's play *Saint Oscar* (1989) concentrates on Wilde the Irishman and imagines a vigorous debate between Wilde and Speranza.

CONTEXT

The Aesthetic movement flourished during the 1880s, and was heavily influenced by the Pre-Raphaelites John Ruskin (1819–1900) and Walter Pater (1839–94). It emphasised the self-sufficiency and importance of art: 'art for art's sake'.

OSCAR WILDE'S LIFE AND WORKS

Oscar Wilde invented celebrity. Before he had written anything of note, he was famous for being himself. Irishman, Christian, aesthete, homosexual, socialist, family man, wit and **dandy**, Wilde made use of every facet of his personality in his work, noting especially: 'I took the drama, the most objective form known to art, and made it as personal a mode of expression as the lyric or the sonnet' (*De Profundis, Complete Works*, p. 1017). Oscar Fingal O'Flahertie Wills Wilde ('not so much a name as a sentence') was born in Dublin on 16 October 1854. His father, Sir William Wilde, was a famous and eccentric eye surgeon; his mother, Jane Elgee, was a noted hostess who wrote passionate Irish Nationalist verse under the name Speranza (the Italian for 'hope'). In addition to two sons and a daughter who died young, William Wilde had three illegitimate children. Wilde had a lifelong fascination with illegitimacy as a theme, although the cheerful acceptance of the fact by all the family was a long way removed from the traumas associated with the subject in *A Woman of No Importance*.

In 1874 Wilde won a scholarship to Magdalen College, Oxford, where he considered his life really began. His major intellectual influences were two academics associated with what was loosely termed the Aesthetic movement. John Ruskin's focus was on art and the education of the oppressed classes, Walter Pater's on the human capacity for intense experience. Both were in revolt against the fussiness, stolidity and commercialism of Victorian style. Wilde rapidly established himself as an Oxford 'character'. He dressed eccentrically (one of his coats was modelled on a cello) and famously remarked: 'I find it difficult to live up to my blue china' (quoted in Ellmann's *Oscar Wilde*, p. 44). He was also a startlingly effective fighter, briskly flooring four tough undergraduates who thought his fancy clothes made him a soft target. Despite a stormy relationship with the university authorities (although he was a brilliant Greek scholar, they disapproved of his taking time out of college to visit Greece), he won the prestigious Newdigate Prize for his poem 'Ravenna' and graduated with a double first in 1878.

In London Wilde struggled to live on a small legacy from his father and published some undistinguished poetry. He also built up a formidable list of famous contacts – including the actress Lillie Langtry, mistress of the Prince of Wales; and the French tragic actress Sarah Bernhardt – and wrote a political **tragedy**, *Vera*. His personality was already his fortune. In 1881 the D'Oyly Carte company planned to take the Gilbert and Sullivan opera *Patience*, a skit on the Aesthetic movement, to the USA. Uncertain whether Americans would understand the humour, they paid Wilde to tour ahead of them giving lectures on Aestheticism. Frustrated that *Vera* was considered too politically sensitive for the English stage, Wilde sailed in December 1881, and docked on 2 January 1882. *Punch* published a cartoon of a weeping maiden languishing on the shore as she waved off the SS *Arizona*.

America boosted Wilde's confidence. He was both wittier and tougher than the droopy hero of *Patience* and worked to establish his own following. During the extensive and exhausting tour he sometimes found the press hostile, but was warmly received by the working class, notably the miners in the Rocky Mountains. *A Woman of No Importance* shows both his liking for the energy and enterprise of the New World and his impatience with its vulgarity and love of money. When he returned in December he was famous; he had secured a New York production for *Vera* and had enough material to tour England for several years giving lectures on 'Experiences in America' and 'The House Beautiful'. During this period of what he called 'civilising the provinces' (quoted in Ellmann's *Oscar Wilde*, p. 232) he married Constance Lloyd and they had two sons, Cyril and Vyvyan. The fairy stories he wrote for them were published as *The Happy Prince and Other Tales* in 1888, eking out his income from lecturing and critical journalism. These were followed by two collections of stories for adults, *A House of Pomegranates* and *Lord Arthur Savile's Crime and Other Stories*, in 1891. In 1887 he also began to earn a regular salary as editor of the *Woman's World*; while he found administration tedious, he transformed the magazine with articles about current

CONTEXT

Lillie Langtry (1853–1929) was a famous beauty nicknamed 'the Jersey Lily'. Wilde flirted with her briefly and they remained friends for many years. Langtry became the mistress of the Prince of Wales, and turned to the stage in order to capitalise on her celebrity; although she was not an actress of much range or depth she had a remarkable stage presence.

CHECK THE BOOK

Walter Satterthwaite's *Wilde West* (1991) is an entertaining novel set during Wilde's American tour, in which Wilde finds himself playing detective. It is rich in precise historical detail.

CONTEXT

Sarah Bernhardt (1844–1923), known as 'the Divine Sarah', was probably the best-known actress of the nineteenth century, performing all over Europe and America. She acted well into old age, even after she lost a leg, and was a pioneer of the silent cinema, playing Hamlet in 1900. In 1892 she met Wilde and suggested he write a play for her. He gave her the script of *Salomé*, and she agreed to play the title role – although Wilde wanted her to play the moon, a part he felt was central to the play. She had begun working on *Salomé* when the censor announced that the play could not be put on.

affairs and women's suffrage (for which Constance was a campaigner); he had always taken seriously the question of women's rights and many of his works, including *A Woman of No Importance*, touch on the matter.

In 1886 Wilde met Robert Ross at Oxford. The young man became his lover, and remained a devoted friend throughout Wilde's lifetime. From that point Wilde led a double life. In 1885 male homosexual activity had been made a criminal offence by the Labouchère Amendment. It was rapidly dubbed 'the blackmailer's charter', as those who had never made efforts to conceal their sexuality suddenly became vulnerable to anyone who knew their secret. Wilde's casual affairs with young men put him at terrible risk; he was well aware of this, as shown by his term for these encounters: 'feasting with panthers' (quoted in Ellmann, p. 367). Increasingly, his work was preoccupied with themes of doubleness, duplicity and the shaping of the self. His only novel, *The Portrait of Dorian Gray*, was published in 1891 and told the story of a young man who, under the malign influence of an older aristocrat, gives up his soul to retain his beauty while his hidden portrait gradually takes on all the marks of age and wickedness. Despite its morality-tale format, its portrayal of what were clearly homosexual relationships made it deeply shocking to the public – although they bought it in large numbers.

Wilde developed ideas expressed in *Dorian Gray* in his essays 'The Critic as Artist' (published in *Intentions*) and *The Soul of Man Under Socialism*, the latter inspired by a speech given by George Bernard Shaw (1856–1950). Here Wilde asserts that everyone – not just the wealthy or the guardians of orthodox morality – has a right and a duty to become an individual: 'he who would lead a Christlike life is he who is perfectly and absolutely himself' (*Complete Works*, p. 1181). It is a standard against which many of the characters he created can be judged and found wanting – not only the overtly wicked, like Dorian Gray, but also those who conform to social expectations against their real natures, like Mrs Arbuthnot in *A Woman of No Importance*. He also wrote another play, *Salomé*, in French; because it portrayed a biblical character it was refused a licence in England.

Disappointed in the royalties for *Dorian Gray*, Wilde turned to the stage as a better source of income and began to write the social **comedies** that would dominate the West End between 1892 and 1895. Widely perceived as the best of their kind for over a hundred years, they all deal with the issues of hypocrisy and authenticity, but in very different ways. In the first of them, *Lady Windermere's Fan*, staged in 1892 at the St James's Theatre, a 'fallen' woman meets her puritanical daughter, who believes her to be dead. She never reveals her identity, but when the daughter gets into a compromising situation her mother takes the blame. The daughter is allowed to keep the illusion of her 'perfect' dead mother, while the real one makes a happy marriage to a rich man and is far less gloomily repentant than the 'fallen' Mrs Arbuthnot in *A Woman of No Importance*.

The conflict between **dandy** and **puritan** in this, Wilde's second comedy, staged at the Haymarket in 1893, leaves the virtuous Hester triumphant over the unrepentant Lord Illingworth. Wilde examined this conflict again, from a fresh angle, in *An Ideal Husband* in 1895. Here the 'fallen' character is a politician who has sold a state secret. He is blackmailed by an unscrupulous woman, but is eventually saved from disgrace and finally forgiven by his puritanical wife. This happy ending is engineered by the most apparently frivolous character on stage, the dandified Lord Goring, who is rewarded with the love of the politician's witty sister. The play opened to critical acclaim at the Haymarket and was still playing when Wilde's greatest comedy, *The Importance of Being Earnest*, opened at the St James's Theatre a month later on 14 February 1895. All the conflicts between image and reality, between men and women, between the aristocracy and the lower orders, between the mask and the self, were crystallised into what Wilde called 'a trivial comedy for serious people'.

Wilde had found his distinctive voice. He was well off, for the first time in his life, having sensibly secured a share of the profits for *Lady Windermere's Fan*. He was also at his most productive. His own secrets, however, could no longer be concealed. He had been introduced to Lord Alfred Douglas, known as Bosie, in 1891; by June 1892 he was in love with him and they spent most of the

CONTEXT

Published in France in 1893, *Salomé* was performed three years later in Paris. In 1894 an English translation by Lord Alfred Douglas (1870–1945) was published, with illustrations by Aubrey Beardsley.

CONTEXT

Lady Windermere's Fan was a great success with critics and audiences alike, creating a profit of seven thousand pounds for Wilde.

CHECK THE BOOK

Regenia Gagnier's *Idylls of the Marketplace: Oscar Wilde and the Victorian Public* (1987) looks at Wilde's relationships with different audiences. It discusses in detail the smart society cliques who attended Wilde's social comedies, and the theatre managements that produced them.

**CHECK
THE FILM**

Oscar Wilde's flamboyant personality and troubled life has given rise to a number of novels, plays and films. Brian Gilbert's 1997 film *Wilde*, starring Stephen Fry as Wilde, is the most recent film about his life and covers his trials in detail.

**CHECK
THE BOOK**

David Hare's play *The Judas Kiss* (1998) focuses on the passionate and destructive relationship between Wilde and Lord Alfred Douglas at two crucial periods – the point when Wilde chose not to escape abroad but face prosecution, and the time they lived together when Wilde was released.

summer together. Like his father, the ninth Marquess of Queensberry, Douglas was dangerously unstable. He drained Wilde financially and had public and spectacular fits of temper; he and Wilde both had other lovers, and while *A Woman of No Importance* was in rehearsal Douglas gave a young man called Alfred Wood a cast-off suit without noticing that it had some letters from Wilde in the pockets. The 'blackmailer's charter' lived up to its name. Wood asked Wilde for some money, and was given fifteen pounds. He then got involved with two professional blackmailers, Allen and Clibborn, who sent a copy of one of the letters to the manager and star of the play, Herbert Beerbohm Tree, at the Haymarket Theatre, along with a demand for money; a mystified Tree warned Wilde to take care. Wilde gently told Allen that if he could, as he claimed, get sixty pounds for the letter from the newspapers he should take it, as the press had never offered him so large a sum for a short piece of prose. Clibborn returned the letter, saying that Wilde was 'kind' and they felt he would 'only laugh' at threats. Wilde complained that they had got the letter dirty and gave Clibborn his fare home.

This was a minor incident, but it indicated that Wilde's private life was becoming harder to conceal as well as to manage. Wilde was finding it increasingly difficult to cope with Douglas' tantrums. Matters came to a head when he gave Douglas the opportunity to translate *Salomé*. Douglas' French was not up to the task, and a violent quarrel ensued when he insisted that his name be published on the final version. Wilde attempted to end the relationship, and Douglas went abroad for a time. However, the situation was fatally complicated by the interference of Queensberry. Douglas was determined to spite his father, and with what *A Woman of No Importance* describes as 'the tyranny of the weak' (Act III, p. 69) made suicide threats and even persuaded Wilde's wife, Constance, to intercede for him with Oscar. Queensberry responded with threats of violence and legal proceedings; perpetually at odds with his family – he divorced his first wife and was estranged from two of his sons – he was in a volatile state after the annulment of his second marriage and the suicide of his son Drumlanrig over a relationship with a member of the Cabinet.

Ironically, Wilde's compassion for Douglas over his brother's death kept them together. Queensberry, who loathed Wilde not only for his sexuality but for his Irish birth and middle-class status, attempted a public demonstration at the triumphant first night of *The Importance of Being Earnest*; thwarted, he left a bouquet of vegetables at the stage door. He went on to leave a card at Wilde's club: 'to Oscar Wilde, posing as a Somdomite' (Queensberry could not spell, and his writing was so bad that the exact words on the card have been disputed ever since). Egged on by Douglas, Wilde tried to sue Queensberry for criminal libel in April 1895, dangerously confident that his wit and style would carry him through. With threats and bribes Queensberry assembled some of Wilde's former lovers and pleaded justification. He won the case and a warrant was issued for Wilde's arrest. For motives that have never been clear, Wilde chose not to do what others in his situation had done: flee to Europe. He underwent two criminal trials on charges of gross indecency and was sentenced to two years in prison with hard labour. Meanwhile he was bankrupted; managers (with the shining exception of Charles Wyndham) took his name off their playbills even before he was convicted and scrambled to buy up the rights of Wilde's plays at knockdown prices. The sensational publicity was more damaging because of Wilde's relationship with his audience: his first nights had resembled grand parties at which he was the host.

While Wilde was in prison his mother, Speranza, died, which caused him great guilt and distress. Constance, herself ill after a serious fall, came to Reading Prison to break the news. Misunderstandings between her family and Wilde's friends meant that he lost the right to see her or the children, and after this meeting Wilde never saw her again, although she supported him financially. Provided with paper by the governor of the jail, Wilde wrote a fifty-thousand-word letter, now known as *De Profundis*, to Douglas, although the text was not published in full until 1962, when both of them were dead.

On Wilde's release in 1897 he travelled to Dieppe under the name Sebastian Melmoth, where he was met by Robert Ross. He was visited by the actor Lugné-Poe, who had staged *Salomé*, but the

---

www. CHECK THE NET

Reading Wilde, Querying Spaces is a website to commemorate the centenary of Wilde's imprisonment, and contains a wealth of visual material from a variety of nineteenth-century publications. Go to **www.nyu.edu** and search for Oscar Wilde.

CONTEXT

Sebastian Melmoth is the character in C. R. Maturin's *Melmoth the Wanderer* (1820). In the novel Sebastian has sold his soul for the promise of prolonged life, and offers other characters relief from their suffering if they will take over his bargain with the devil.

British community were unwelcoming and he moved to the more secluded town of Berneval. Here he wrote letters of thanks to those friends who had supported him, including Mrs Bernard Beere, who had played Mrs Arbuthnot in *A Woman of No Importance*. 'Suffering is a terrible fire,' he wrote to her, 'it either purifies or destroys; perhaps I may be a better fellow after it all' (*The Letters of Oscar Wilde*, edited by Rupert Hart-Davies, 1963). He began work, writing a letter to the *Daily Chronicle* about prison conditions, and demanding the reinstatement of a warder, Thomas Martin. Martin had been kind to Wilde and lost his job for giving a child prisoner a biscuit. He also finished *The Ballad of Reading Gaol*, his best poem, based on the story of a fellow prisoner hanged for murder. It was published in 1898 under the name C.3.3., Wilde's prison number. Briefly, he lived with Douglas in Naples, although aware that he was being exploited and that his relations with Constance were being further damaged.

Wilde's last days were spent travelling Europe, poor and in increasingly bad health, although he outlived Constance, and visited her grave in Genoa in April 1899. Towards the end of 1899 he became seriously ill of meningitis in Paris and complained that he was 'dying, as he had lived, beyond his means' (Morley, *Oscar Wilde*, p. 149). He was baptised into the Catholic Church and received the last rites (he could no longer speak; his friends were not sure whether the desire he had previously expressed for this was genuine – his beliefs were hardly orthodox – but they decided to go ahead). On 30 November 1900 he died, with Ross at his side. Despite some disparaging obituaries, his reputation as a writer was soon restored. By 1909 continental productions of the plays had paid off his debts and his body was transferred to Père Lachaise Cemetery among artists and writers; by 1914 all his **comedies** had been revived on the London stage.

HISTORICAL BACKGROUND

THE STATE OF THE NATION

Fin de siècle, fin du globe. The end of an era (literally 'end of century'), the end of the world. Sarcastically quoted by Lord Illingworth towards the end of the play (Act IV, p. 110), the phrase *fin de siècle* was used by many writers of the 1890s – including Wilde himself on more than one occasion. It reminds the audience that even in this apparently idyllic country retreat it is impossible to shut out the concerns of the wider world. The end of any century leads people to ask questions about the state of the world and their nation in particular; and the Victorians, with the queen who had reigned since she was eighteen now in her seventies, saw the 1890s, as Illingworth does here, as a period of transition and decay.

Britain controlled an empire from which wealth poured in to make it the richest nation in the world. However, the United States, independent from Britain for a hundred years and trading with other nations on equal rather than colonial terms, was not far behind; the difference in outlook and policy between the two countries was a source of continual interest and discussion. A particular concern at this time was that without some sort of import controls to favour empire traders, America might damage British commercial interests. Hester's presence as the daughter of an American millionaire is significant, especially as her father is a philanthropist. The self-made super-rich of the United States had the power to create schools, universities, libraries – and in doing so they could change people's lives without reference to a rigid class system. Hester is free to use her money how she likes, and she creates the family that she wants; Lord Illingworth cannot, in the end, do this for his son and the mother of his child, even if they wished it, because the complex structure of aristocratic inheritance forbids it.

The presence of an independent young woman with wealth earned through trade also opens up a wider debate; the English characters cannot help knowing that their world will have to change. For in Britain the gap between rich and poor was widening dangerously. In the wake of a series of agricultural depressions, rural labourers poured into the towns looking for work, until the urban population almost doubled. This led to overcrowding – the term 'slum' was used for the first time in the nineteenth century – which led to bad sanitation, disease and destitution. The term 'unemployment' was also coined in the 1880s; the unemployed themselves rioted in Trafalgar Square in 1886 and 1887 and were brutally suppressed.

 **CHECK THE BOOK**

Judith R. Walkowitz's *City of Dreadful Delight: Narratives of Sexual Danger in Late-Victorian London* (1992) examines late Victorian anxieties about gender in relation to the darker side of London life.

The notorious Whitechapel murders by Jack the Ripper in 1888 were perceived as a consequence of poverty and neglect. Research over the period suggested that almost thirty per cent of the population did not earn enough to keep their families fed and clothed. With the country as a whole for the first time really aware of the problem, something needed to be done. Existing schemes for the welfare of the poor had never been designed to cope on such a large scale. However, the political parties were unable to agree on a solution. Conservative reforms failed to satisfy, while the Liberals were hopelessly divided on policy. Two possibilities originally proposed by Chamberlain's radical wing of the Liberal party in 1885 – to give the vote to all adult males and to reform or abolish the House of Lords – are discussed in the play. Lady Hunstanton finds the first of these shocking (Act I, p. 18), and universal male suffrage was not achieved until after 1914 (for women it took even longer). In the play, only the Archdeacon and Mr Kelvil would be able to vote – everyone else is a woman, an aristocrat, too young, or a servant without property qualifications. Kelvil tentatively enquires whether Lord Illingworth thinks the Lords is 'a better institution' than the Commons (Act I, p. 19); he perhaps sees the aristocracy as an endangered species.

> **CONTEXT**
>
> As calls for the abolition of the House of Lords increased during the 1880s, the militantly Tory Lord Curzon declared in words rather like Illingworth's: 'All civilisation has been the work of aristocracies.'

Even among radicals of the 1890s, there was a widespread distrust of socialism and a strong resistance to taxing the better off to relieve the situation of the poor. Hence the debates about poverty in the play reflect pressing realities of class conflict. Some of the wealthier characters, such as Lady Caroline and the Archdeacon, still think that the solution lies in private charity, some of it administered by the Church. The suggestion that all the poor really need is 'Blankets and coals' (Act I, p. 19) would sound familiar to Wilde's audience; there were many charitable organisations with specific aims about the provision of clothes, household equipment or Bibles. However, such charity could become little more than a hobby for the rich. Here giving blankets and coals is seen as no more necessary or virtuous than Lady Hunstanton's gift of a brace of partridges to the wealthy invalid Mrs Daubeny (Act III, p. 78).

Lord Illingworth delights in shocking the company with radical pronouncements. When Kelvil praises the House of Commons for its 'great sympathy with the sufferings of the poor', he responds: 'That is its special vice' (Act I, p. 18). However, Wilde expressed similar sentiments in all seriousness in *The Soul of Man Under Socialism* (1891). In this essay he says that it is the state's responsibility to help every individual develop freely after it has made an end to 'the misery and rage and depression produced by our wrong system of property-holding' (*Complete Works*, p. 1182). In the years immediately preceding the birth of the Labour Party, some at least of Wilde's audience might have shared this view; many of them would have recognised it; most of them would have enjoyed the **paradox** of hearing it from the mouth of Illingworth, a member of the idle rich.

THE ANGEL IN THE HOUSE

Wilde chose the title of *A Woman of No Importance* carefully: the position of women was an issue of considerable importance throughout the nineteenth century, and much imaginative literature was produced on the subject. By the last decade of the century major changes were happening in the face of considerable resistance. Prevalent among the professions to which women were forbidden access – government, the law, the Church, the universities, medicine – was the idea of the two or separate spheres. This was the notion that men and women were spiritually and biologically designed to operate in different worlds – men in the world at large, and women in the home. 'Man for the sword and for the needle she', as Lord Tennyson put it in his poem *The Princess* (1847).

Women gradually brought about change by their own efforts. Colleges were founded at the end of the 1840s and universities admitted women – although it was not until the next century that they were awarded degrees. Women became nurses, doctors and teachers, and some of their activity in the charitable field went far beyond the sphere of 'Blankets and coals' (Act I, p. 19) to accomplish major social reforms. However, they constantly risked not just opposition but the accusation that they were unnatural and unhealthy. For working-class women, life was physically exhausting. They not only worked long hours in factories and mills but had total responsibility for the home and the care of their children. For the better off, like the women in Wilde's play, the

---

CONTEXT

The Labour Representation Committee (LRC) was formed in 1900 as a result of the combined efforts of the trade unions, the cooperative societies and socialist parties such as the Independent Labour Party. Six years later, the Labour Party was formally established.

CHECK THE BOOK

The Angel in the House is a sequence of poems written by Coventry Patmore (1823–96) between 1854 and 1862. In this work he writes about the ideal Victorian wife and woman, who should be devoted and obedient to her husband: 'Man must be pleased; but to him to please / Is woman's pleasure'.

CONTEXT

In 1931 Virginia Woolf gave a lecture entitled 'Professions for Women' to the Women's Service League in which she described the pressure exerted by the 'Angel in the House'. Woolf said that a woman with ambitions to write needed to kill the Angel, and admitted that she imagined strangling her and throwing inkpots at her head on a regular basis.

pressures were largely psychological: a wife who did not work was the visible proof of her husband's success. Girls were often denied education beyond skills such as music, dancing and embroidery which might help catch a husband, and those who did manage to learn were expected to keep the fact quiet. A manual called *The Wives of England* (c.1843) recommended that the woman should 'show by the most delicate attentions how much she feels her husband's superiority to herself'. Lady Hunstanton is showing herself as a proper product of Victorian education when she says: 'I have very little to reproach myself with, on the score of thinking. I don't believe in women thinking too much' (Act III, p. 77).

One way in which the two spheres were distinguished was that the world of work was seen as competitive and aggressive, and the home as a place of quiet spirituality. The wife was the guardian of piety and morality for the whole family – what a poem in the 1850s called 'the Angel in the House'. The Angel was understood to be 'naturally' unselfish, always putting her family first. This made it easier for legislation to treat her as an extension of her husband rather than an individual. Until the Married Women's Property Acts were passed – a process which took place in a piecemeal and begrudging fashion, in 1870, 1882, 1884 and 1893, making the discussion in Act II highly topical – a wife could own nothing, not even property inherited from her own parents or money she had earned from her own work; she was not seen as needing anything for herself.

Mrs Arbuthnot's reputation as a 'sweet saint' (Act IV, p. 90) whose domestic style reflects her virtues shows not so much her character as her success in conforming to the Angel image. Her very frank admission of enjoyment and desire for the 'pleasant things of life' (Act IV, p. 99) is a radical statement. The Angel could not have many active virtues; her speciality was a passive purity. Purity in a woman was considered to be important as it guaranteed the paternity of a man's children: it was taken for granted that men should be judged with greater leniency because 'their temptations were greater and their resistance less', as Caroline Norton put it in her *English Laws for Women in the Nineteenth Century* of 1854.

Hester is unusual in her demand that men and women should be seen as equally guilty in a sexual sin.

Received wisdom also stated that women did not feel sexual desire. It is not only the seasoned flirts in the play, cheerfully admitting to illicit relationships and to disappointment with their husbands, who imply that this is far from the truth: Mrs Arbuthnot, when she tells Illingworth that 'A kiss may ruin a human life' (Act IV, p. 104), sadly acknowledges her own complicity in their love affair. But the idea that women felt no sexual urges was so firmly entrenched that it made possible sweeping judgements such as those made by Gerald and Hester. They have been reared to be 'innocent' – dangerously ignorant. For Hester her evident lack of sexual *savoir faire* means that Lord Illingworth's overtures at the end of Act III come as a terrifying shock, and she is not confident enough to reject him without Gerald's intervention; for Gerald it means that he cannot imagine a 'nice' girl giving in to Illingworth – although, arguably, a girl less innocent than Rachel might have been less inclined to take his promises seriously.

'Fallen' women both inside and outside marriage were treated hypocritically. Prostitution was called 'the great social evil'; the number of prostitutes was estimated by some to be as high as 368,000. Women rather than men campaigned for their welfare and saw that the age of consent was raised to sixteen in 1885. Many unmarried mothers found themselves drifting into prostitution; others ended up in one of the 'admirable homes where people of that kind are looked after and reformed', as Lady Hunstanton cheerfully puts it (Act III, p. 76) – perhaps unaware that in many of them conditions were harsh to the point of cruelty. After the Matrimonial Causes Act of 1857, secular divorce was possible, but again the double standard prevailed. A wife had to find evidence of other marital failings besides adultery, such as cruelty or desertion. She might have custody of her very young children or access to those over seven, but it was not until 1925 that she had an equal right to be guardian of her own child. A husband could divorce his wife for adultery and she would lose all chance of custody of the children. For all her troubles, Mrs Arbuthnot, who seems lucky enough to have an independent income, is in a far better situation than a 'fallen' wife.

CONTEXT

The fourth Married Women's Property Act was passed in the same year as the premiere of *A Woman of No Importance* (1893). Prior to these acts, a man took complete ownership of all his wife's property upon marriage and kept it if they divorced. One notorious case of the early nineteenth century, that of writer and reformer Caroline Norton (1808–77), saw a woman who left a violent man treated as 'legally non-existent' (because husband and wife were considered 'one person'), denied the right to see her children and forced to give her husband the money she had earned by writing when he had refused to support her.

THE NEW WOMAN

The term 'New Woman' was coined by the novelist Sarah Grand (1854–1943) in 1894 to name a figure already visible in English and American society, a figure who transcends the views of what Grand called 'the Bawling Brotherhood' of men wishing to hold women back. The media struggled to define the New Woman, but by and large agreed that she was one who was eager to take advantage of the new opportunities for education and work and might well have a profession. She might choose not to marry, and would not see herself as a failure without a husband. She cared about her own health and played sports rather than looking elegantly feeble – this was the golden age of the bicycle. She dressed in clothes that allowed freedom of movement – Constance Wilde was a member of the Rational Dress Society, doing without bustles and corsets and even wearing trousers among friends. She would probably campaign for the vote and take an active part in politics.

Hester's views suggest that she might accept the New Woman label for herself. She is interested in politics and vocal on the subject; she admires people who work (although she does not do any); she controls her own money; and she has no inhibitions about virtually proposing marriage to Gerald and deciding that his mother will live with them. Her views on sexual equality are progressive, although she is more conventional, at least at the beginning of the play, in her views about sex; some of her contemporaries might well challenge the institutions of marriage and the family. Wilde makes fun of Hester's naivety, but he allows her to grow up in the course of the play, and at the close she has arguably redefined the idea of family and shown herself to be more progressive than the aristocrats who merely pretend to conform to social norms.

LITERARY AND THEATRICAL BACKGROUND

GENERAL INFLUENCES

Wilde liked to discount the idea that he was subject to influence, and only admitted to it in the most flippant way – as when he asserted that the plot of *A Woman of No Importance* was taken from a story in the *Family Herald*. This was not so much arrogance as a reflection of the breadth and variety of his knowledge: he not only drew from many sources; he combined them to make something that was very much his own.

He was not, however, greatly in sympathy with the **realism** that characterised the novels with which he grew up and which still predominated. The Victorian novel tended to examine in psychological detail characters from a wide social spectrum but within a specific range of experience – courtship, marriage, money and family. While it might explore social problems or even call for particular reforms, it did not demand a change in thinking. The problems of the 'fallen' woman, for example, were often treated with sympathy – for instance by Charles Dickens in *David Copperfield* (1949–50) and Elizabeth Gaskell in *Ruth* (1853) – but not in a way that challenged contemporary notions of sexuality. Usually the woman redeemed herself through a life of piety. Even this was not enough to diminish the shock for some readers: Gaskell's husband forbade her to read her own novel. Thomas Hardy shocked the nation with his 1891 novel *Tess of the D'Urbervilles: A Pure Woman*, which showed a 'fallen' woman driven to murder and despair; and the reception of his next book, *Jude the Obscure* (1895), which dwelt on the disastrous consequences of a bad marriage and the strains of extramarital relationships, led him to give up writing novels.

Various schools of thought, often merging into one another, shifted the paradigms of realism a little. The Decadent movement in France urged poets and writers to look at the unusual, the ugly, the sexually dissident and the marginal, and to embrace the artificial and urban rather than the natural. In England the spirit of the decadents produced a number of journals, of which the most famous was the *Yellow Book* (1894–6); its best-known artist was the young Aubrey Beardsley (1872–98), who illustrated *Salomé*; his drawings, elegantly unfussy next to the obsessive detail of popular Victorian painters, are often grotesque and sexually explicit. The Decadent movement had an impact on the Aesthetic school of Walter Pater, who taught Wilde at Oxford. Pater's *Studies in the History of the Renaissance* (1873) proclaimed that art should not provide a moral vision but intensity of experience for its own sake. Wilde's essay 'The Decay of

www. CHECK THE NET

The Theatre Museum has an excellent online guided tour to the Victorian theatre, including posters, photographs, biographies, reviews and audio clips. Go to **www. peopleplayuk.org. uk** and click on Guided Tours, then Drama and 19th Century Theatre.

CONTEXT

The Decadent school often linked images of exotic flowers with the idea of sin. A famous line from Algernon Charles Swinburne's poem 'Dolores' (1866) speaks of 'The lilies and languors of virtue / For the rapture and roses of vice'. Wilde makes fun of this when Mrs Allonby mentions 'an orchid ... as beautiful as the seven deadly sins', and Lady Hunstanton replies: 'I will certainly speak to the gardener' (Act I, pp. 20–1).

CHECK THE BOOK

There is a witty account of Ruskin's road and Wilde's part in building it in Tom Stoppard's play about the poet A. E. Housman, Wilde's contemporary, *The Invention of Love* (1997).

CONTEXT

Wilde wrote of Meredith in his essay 'The Decay of Lying': 'Who can define him? His style is chaos illumined by flashes of lightning' (*Complete Works*, p. 1076). Meredith's novel *The Egoist*, published in 1879, contained rapid-fire battles of wit between the sexes; he claimed he had been inspired to write it working on his 1877 lecture. His 1885 novel *Diana of the Crossways* created an unconventional and modern heroine.

Lying' similarly asserted that art should not imitate life. The popular press loved to present an image of Wilde as 'one of the high priests of the decadent school which attacks all the wholesome, manly, simple ideals of English life' (the words of the *Evening News* during Wilde's trial). But Wilde's anti-**realism** was not simplistic; if he celebrated artifice he could also mock it in his plays and add a political edge. At Oxford he not only attended with enthusiasm John Ruskin's lectures on art as a force *of* good and *for* good, but participated in his bizarre experiment to assert the dignity of labour by building a road. (It sank.) He never lost an acute awareness of Victorian sexual hypocrisy or its indifference to poverty. His novel *The Picture of Dorian Gray* celebrates the passion for beauty and the value of homosexual love, but also shows its hero abusing his power to seduce a girl from a poor family. Like the most famous late Victorian parable of doubleness, Robert Louis Stevenson's *The Strange Case of Dr Jekyll and Mr Hyde* (1886), it uses fantasy to explore the damage caused by the need to preserve an acceptable public face.

As an Irishman Wilde was also aware of a line of distinguished predecessors who critiqued English politics and culture through their beguiling command of the language. He learned most from the witty Irish exponents of the **comedy of manners**: George Farquhar and William Congreve at the beginning of the eighteenth century and Richard Sheridan and Oliver Goldsmith towards its end. In a world where marriages were arranged on an economic basis, their plays showed lovers negotiating both sanctioned and illicit liaisons, struggling with the pains of desire and the risks of loving in a world where divorce was impossible and women's rights minimal. The jokes were verbal rather than visual, the language of the couples a sophisticated battle of wits which playfully postponed the moment of surrender. A popular feature was the **proviso scene** in which the woman spelled out to the man the conditions under which she might accept him – generally privacy, fidelity and equality. Beneath the playfulness of this drama lies an undercurrent of sadness, the playwrights vividly aware that the world in which these fabulous wits move involves war, disease and poverty. The most famous Victorian exponent of the comedy of manners was the novelist, poet and critic George Meredith (1828–1909), whose lecture of 1877 on

'The Idea of Comedy' was widely circulated; he maintained that true comedy depended on a degree of equality between men and women. Certainly Wilde's witty flirts are at their best and the comedy most light-hearted when the competition is even.

THEATRICAL INFLUENCES

Victorian theatre was a lavish spectacle. Behind the **fourth wall** of a **proscenium arch** it offered images which gave the audience an illusion of reality. Plots might test credulity, language could be strained and extravagant, but sophisticated backstage technology and cheap labour could be combined to produce extraordinary effects: train crashes, chariot races – even sinking ships looked realistic. **Melodrama** – originally devised because until 1843 only a restricted number of theatres were allowed to stage plays, while musical interludes allowed a piece to be defined as a 'burletta' – offered straightforward plots full of cliffhanging **suspense**. Sustaining its popularity among the working and lower middle classes throughout the nineteenth century, melodrama was often grounded in powerful images of class struggle – landlord versus tenant, honest working man against aristocrat, simple girl against manipulative rich seducer. Wilde's exploration of class conflict – and indeed his careful use of Hester's violin to underscore a key scene – suggests that he was well aware of the power of the form. As the century drew on there was a conscious attempt by managements to woo the wealthier classes into the West End with more luxurious decor, comfortable seating and electric light (all of which meant higher prices). This exclusive theatre perceived its drama as more subtle and realistic, although from a twenty-first-century perspective it is perhaps the similarities with melodrama rather than the differences which strike us.

The format for what the Victorian theatre called the **well-made play** (a play with a precise structure consisting of **exposition, developments and complications, crisis** and **resolution** across three or four acts, each with an exciting curtain) was laid down by the French dramatists Eugène Scribe (1791–1861) and Victorien Sardou (1831–1908). Their own plays in fact closely resembled popular melodrama. One native English strain that developed the well-made format was the sentimental social **comedy** of middle-class life for

---

CONTEXT

Scribe's first play appeared in 1815; he wrote at least five hundred during his lifetime. He coined the term *pièce bien faite* (well-made play) to describe the formula he recommended to discipline the often very extravagant and emotional style of the drama of his time. His disciple Sardou developed the format and it was enormously influential in the theatre of the nineteenth century (too influential for the taste of George Bernard Shaw, who coined the term 'Sardoodledom'). Their plays are virtually unknown now – except for a version of one work of Sardou, which is played all over the world as the opera *Tosca*.

CONTEXT

The Alexandre Dumas who wrote *Le Fils naturel* (known as Dumas *fils*) is not to be confused with the Alexandre Dumas famous for *Le Comte de Monte Cristo* (1844–5) and *Les Trois mousquetaires* (1844) – his father.

CHECK THE BOOK

Kerry Powell's *Oscar Wilde and the Theatre of the 1890s* (1990) suggests that all Wilde's plays have their roots in the works of other writers, especially the French dramas of the previous generation. Powell draws detailed comparisons between *A Woman of No Importance* and Dumas' play *Le Fils naturel*, although he does not dwell on the differences in tone.

which T. W. Robertson was famous in the mid-century. But there was also a continuing interest in the French **boulevard drama** that evolved over the first half of the century. This dealt with issues of legitimacy, marital betrayal, jealousy and seduction, and revenge and blackmail. The central character was often a 'woman with a past'. One play that closely resembles *A Woman of No Importance* in terms of its basic situation is Alexandre Dumas' *Le Fils naturel*, written in 1858 and staged in London in 1890. In it the illegitimate son of a sweet and humble servant girl cast off by an aristocrat wants to marry his father's niece; the aristocrat refuses. His son becomes a national hero and shames his father by having him made a count, while his mother is happy to remain sweetly in the background so as not to compromise her son. The last scene shows the young couple united and both calling her 'mother', while the humbled aristocrat asks if he may now claim the title 'father'. Wilde saw it at the Gaiety Theatre starring Sarah Bernhardt.

PROBLEM PLAYS

The England of the 1890s, with all its anxiety about gender roles, inevitably embraced the French dramas, but it did so with some timidity. For one of the most important influences on the playwrights of the time was not a writer but the censor. The Theatre Regulation Act of 1843 allowed more theatres to stage spoken drama but tightened censorship; scripts had to be scrutinised by the Lord Chamberlain's Office. Some regulations were clear – there was an absolute ban on biblical subjects, for example. But on the whole the playwright was at the mercy of the censor's interpretation of what might be blasphemous, obscene or corrupting. An examiner of plays could demand that specific words or scenes be cut or changed, or ban a play altogether. There was no appeal. Inevitably there were inconsistencies in examiners' judgements: one might allow a saucy joke but forbid a serious discussion of a social problem; another might allow a well-known writer more freedom than one making his debut. Henry James complained that the situation of the English playwright was the most undignified in Europe. It was inevitable that writers became less adventurous. English plots were less shocking than their French counterparts, replacing adultery with flirtation, or seduction with a temptation resisted. They showed their well-to-do audience an onstage environment very much like their own, dealing with the problems of money and marriage in tastefully appointed drawing-room sets which earned them the label of 'pink lampshade plays'.

However, the well-made form still offered an opportunity to explore serious questions. The Norwegian dramatist Henrik Ibsen did just that in his play *A Doll's House*. Even the censored English theatre could not ignore it. *A Doll's House*, written in 1879, showed a woman, Nora, leaving a marriage in which she has always been treated like a child; her last act is to slam the door. The sound of that door haunted a Europe in which the rights of women were constantly being debated. While one examiner of plays stated that 'all the characters in Ibsen's plays appear to me to be morally deranged', Ibsen's plays were championed in England by George Bernard Shaw and by the influential private organisation the Independent Theatre, which included many women who later formed the Actresses' Franchise League and staged their own plays about women's rights. A sanitised version of *A Doll's House* called *Breaking a Butterfly*, by Henry Arthur Jones, was performed in 1884. The heroine, renamed Flossie, walked back through the famous door to make up with her husband.

In 1889 the original *A Doll's House* was staged, and its impact was considerable. Though some of Ibsen's other plays, notably *Ghosts*, which dealt with syphilis, were banned, there were Ibsen societies dedicated to private readings, and the idea that a **well-made play** could be constructed around a serious social issue took root. George Bernard Shaw wrote 'problem plays' about issues such as slum landlords (*Widowers' Houses*) and prostitution (*Mrs Warren's Profession*). Wilde sent him a copy of *Salomé*, greeting him as a fellow Irishman in 'a land of intellectual fog'. Shaw was working largely in the private independent theatres; Wilde remained in the commercial sphere. While his own work certainly echoed Ibsen's in its implicit concern for the position of women and its scorn of hypocrisy, Wilde did not admire Ibsen's naturalism. His commitment to artificiality allowed him to remain in the West End, among the wealthy. The more radical characters and situations in Wilde's plays led him to be occasionally identified as an Ibsenite – notably in reviews of *A Woman of No Importance*. But his wit

CONTEXT

Ibsen (1828–1906) developed a **naturalistic** style with characters who had a new psychological complexity and moved in a recognisable world – although his construction owed a great deal to Scribe and Sardou. In Britain he was admired by Shaw and theatre innovators for his plays dealing with social problems. The British production of *A Doll's House* in 1889 with the fiery Janet Achurch as Nora at the small and dingy Novelty Theatre proved to be one of the most influential events in the British theatre. The critic Clement Scott rapidly coined the word 'Ibsenite' as a term of abuse.

CONTEXT

When Charles II came to the throne in 1660, theatre had been forbidden for nearly two decades. Cautiously it was restored, but initially only two playhouses – in Drury Lane and Covent Garden – were given the royal patent to stage plays. However, the patent only applied to 'legitimate' drama, and this rapidly came to mean 'non-musical'. Minor theatres mushroomed, staging works they claimed were not technically plays but musical events. Burletta (from the Italian *burla*, meaning 'joke') was a term coined to cover an entertainment that did not want to be considered 'legitimate' drama.

ensured that he maintained his reputation as an entertainer. His particular brand of subversion worked from within.

It is illuminating to compare *A Woman of No Importance* with a play that opened just months later: Sir Arthur Pinero's much admired *The Second Mrs Tanqueray*. In it a woman with a 'past' marries and lives a secluded life, hoping to live it down. When her ex-lover becomes engaged to her stepdaughter Ellean, she persuades her husband to forbid the marriage, and the stepdaughter deduces the truth. The shame is too much for Mrs Tanqueray, who takes poison, while Ellean cries (according to the stage directions, '*beating her breast*'): 'If I had only been merciful!' The play is deeply sympathetic to Mrs Tanqueray's plight, but nobody suggests that she is not really in need of mercy and that there is no real reason why the marriage should not take place. Wilde cheerfully allowed a 'fallen' woman in *Lady Windermere's Fan* to find a husband. There is no marriage between Lord Illingworth and Mrs Arbuthnot – but that is because she refuses to satisfy the proprieties at the cost of spiritual misery, not because she does not 'deserve' to marry him.

WILDE'S INFLUENCE

For many, Wilde's reputation as a writer of brilliant **comedy** tended to mask the fact that he was more radical than his commercial rivals. The assumption that he was somehow wasting his talent in creating an artificial world for the pleasure of the West End persisted for a long time. Vincent O'Sullivan voiced a typical view that 'Wilde lost the chance of being a pioneer. He left it to Bernard Shaw and Archer with his translations of Ibsen' (quoted in Beckson, *Oscar Wilde: The Critical Heritage*, p. 385). But Wilde's playfulness with the idea of identity was a profound influence on another playwright concerned with gender and identity: Noël Coward (1899–1973). From the 1920s to the 1960s, Coward marketed his own personality, shrewdly changing it to fit the changing times, and exploded gender stereotypes in comedies such as *Private Lives* in 1930. As censorship drew to a close in the 1960s, Joe Orton (1933–67) satirised the English preoccupation with respectability in intricate dark comedies such as *What the Butler Saw* (1969), involving rape, incest and illegitimacy. Orton's characters have the Wildean love of **paradox** and crafted language – but he pointed out that Wilde's language was not just a 'glittering style' but revealed the truth of his characters' preoccupation with money and position. Playwrights of the late twentieth and early twenty-first centuries as diverse as Howard Brenton (b.1942) and Tom Stoppard (b.1937) acknowledge Wilde's influence, and in 1998 Mark Ravenhill's *Handbag* (subtitle *The Importance of Being Someone*) plundered the plot of *The Importance of Being Earnest* to create a farce about class relationships, dissident sexualities and – just like *A Woman of No Importance* – the possibility of a family grounded in love rather than conventional parent-child roles. His combination of self-conscious artifice and play and a serious consideration of class and gender relations means that Wilde remains a potent force in the theatre.

CONTEXT

Coward wrote a song – 'Blasé boys are we' – for his operetta *Bitter Sweet* (1929), in which a quartet of dissipated noblemen pay homage to Wilde while wearing Wilde's trademark green carnation.

CHECK THE BOOK

A Companion to Modern British and Irish Drama: 1880–2005, edited by Mary Luckhurst (2006), gives helpful contextualisation by grouping Wilde with a number of comic dramatists. Richard Allen Cave's chapter on Wilde explores the political dimensions of his comedy, arguing that as an Irishman he **satirised** the English upper class through several different kinds of comic style.

World events

1815 Napoleon defeated at Waterloo

1837 Accession of Queen Victoria

1845 Famine in Ireland

1847 Factory Act establishes ten-hour day for women and young males

1848 Uprising in Ireland; revolution in France

1849 Bedford College for Women founded in London

1851 Great Exhibition at Crystal Palace, Hyde Park

1854 Britain enters Crimean War

Oscar Wilde's life

1815 Sir William Wilde born

1826 Jane Francesca Elgee born

1850 Marriage of William Wilde and Jane Elgee

1854 Born in Dublin

Literary events

1815 Eugène Scribe begins writing plays

1843 Theatre Regulation Act

1847 Charlotte Brontë, *Jane Eyre*

1848 Karl Marx and Friedrich Engels, *Communist Manifesto*; Pre-Raphaelite Brotherhood founded by Dante Gabriel Rossetti, William Holman Hunt and Sir John Everett Millais

1849 Charles Dickens, *David Copperfield*

1850 Nathaniel Hawthorne, *The Scarlet Letter*

1852 Charles Morton builds Canterbury Music Hall

1853 Elizabeth Gaskell, *Ruth*

1854 Charles Dickens, *Hard Times*

World events

1857 Matrimonial Causes Act establishes secular divorce in England

1858 Fenian (Irish Republican) Brotherhood founded

1861 American Civil War begins

1864 Contagious Diseases Act

1865 President Abraham Lincoln assassinated

1867 Second Reform Act gives vote to some of male working class

1868 February Benjamin Disraeli becomes prime minister; **December** William Gladstone becomes prime minister

1870 Married Women's Property Act

Oscar Wilde's life

Literary events

1854–62 Coventry Patmore, *The Angel in the House*

1859 Charles Darwin, *On the Origin of Species by Means of Natural Selection*

1862 Mary Elizabeth Braddon, *Lady Audley's Secret*

1865 Lewis Carroll, *Alice in Wonderland*

1867 T. W. Robertson, *Caste*

1869 John Stuart Mill, *On the Subjection of Women*

World events

1871 Trade unions given legal recognition; Paris Commune suppressed

1874 Disraeli wins major election victory and leads Conservative reforming government

1876 Alexander Graham Bell invents telephone

1877 Thomas Edison invents phonograph

1880 Gladstone's second ministry begins; Mundella's Act makes education compulsory for children aged between five and ten

1882 Married Women's Property Act

1885 Labouchère Amendment criminalises consenting homosexual acts in private

Oscar Wilde's life

1871 Wins scholarship to Trinity College, Dublin

1874 Goes to Oxford

1875 Visits Italy

1876 Death of father

1877 Visits Greece

1878 Graduates with double first and wins Newdigate Prize for Poetry

1880 *Vera* published

1881 *Poems* published

1882 US lecture tour

1884 Marries Constance Lloyd

1885 Son Cyril born

Literary events

1874 T. A. Palmer's dramatisation of Mrs Henry Wood's *East Lynne* staged; Impressionist exhibition

1877 Henry James, *The American*; George Meredith's lecture on 'The Idea of Comedy'

1878 William Gilbert and Arthur Sullivan, *HMS Pinafore*

1880 Electric light in the theatre used for first time; Émile Zola, *Naturalism in the Theatre*

1881 Henrik Ibsen, *Ghosts*; Gilbert and Sullivan, *Patience*; Henry James, *The Portrait of a Lady*

1884 Henry Arthur Jones, *Breaking a Butterfly*

World events

1886 Gladstone resigns; Joseph Chamberlain splits the Liberal Party

1888 Match girls' strike; Whitechapel (Jack the Ripper) murders

1892 Gladstone returns to office as prime minister

1893 Married Women's Property Act; formation of Independent Labour Party

1894 Gladstone resigns; Sarah Grand coins term 'New Woman'

Oscar Wilde's life

1886 Son Vyvyan born; meets Robert Ross

1887 Becomes editor of *Woman's World*

1888 *The Happy Prince and Other Tales*

1891 *A House of Pomegranates*; *Lord Arthur Savile's Crime and Other Stories*; *Intentions*; *The Soul of Man Under Socialism*; *The Picture of Dorian Gray*; *Salomé* composed in French; meets Lord Alfred Douglas

1892 *Lady Windermere's Fan* staged; *Salomé* refused licence

1893 *A Woman of No Importance* staged; blackmail attempt on Wilde fails; *Salomé* published in France

1894 Poem *The Sphinx*; English translation of *Salomé* published

Literary events

1886 Robert Louis Stevenson, *The Strange Case of Dr Jekyll and Mr Hyde*

1889 Henrik Ibsen's *A Doll's House* staged in England

1891 Thomas Hardy, *Tess of the D'Urbervilles*; J. T. Grein founds Independent Theatre Club

1892 Charlotte Perkins Gilman, 'The Yellow Wallpaper'; George Bernard Shaw, *Widowers' Houses*; Eugène Brieux, *Monsieur de Réboval*

1893 Sir Arthur Pinero's *The Second Mrs Tanqueray* staged; George Bernard Shaw writes *Mrs Warren's Profession* but censor refuses to license it

1894 First issue of *Yellow Book*

World events	Oscar Wilde's life	Literary events
	1895 *An Ideal Husband* staged; *The Importance of Being Earnest* staged; sues Marquess of Queensberry for libel; Wilde tried for 'gross indecency' and sentenced to two years' hard labour	**1895** Thomas Hardy, *Jude the Obscure*
	1896 Death of mother; *Salomé* performed in Paris; writes *De Profundis*	**1896** Anton Chekhov, *The Seagull*
1897 Queen Victoria's Diamond Jubilee	**1897** Released from prison and moves to France	
	1898 *The Ballad of Reading Gaol* published under name C.3.3.; Constance Wilde dies	**1898** Stanislavsky founds Moscow Arts Theatre
1899–1902 Second Boer War		**1899** Noël Coward born; Anton Chekhov's *Uncle Vanya* staged
	1900 Dies 30 November in Paris	**1900** Henry Arthur Jones, *Mrs Dane's Defence*; Giacomo Puccini's *Tosca* staged
1901 Death of Queen Victoria		
	1905 Partial publication of *De Profundis*	
	1908 First collected works published	
1967 Repeal of the Labouchère Amendment		

FURTHER READING

SELECTED WORKS BY OSCAR WILDE

Lady Windermere's Fan (1892), New Mermaids (reprinted 2006)

An Ideal Husband (1895), New Mermaids (reprinted 2006)

The Importance of Being Earnest (1895), New Mermaids (reprinted 2006)

Other works, including *The Picture of Dorian Gray*, *Salomé*, *De Profundis* and *The Soul of Man Under Socialism*, can be found in the *Complete Works of Oscar Wilde*, edited by Merlin Holland, Collins, 1994 (fifth edition, 2003)

The Letters of Oscar Wilde, edited by Rupert Hart-Davies, Hart-Davies, 1963

BIOGRAPHY

Richard Ellmann, *Oscar Wilde*, Hamish Hamilton, 1987

Sheridan Morley, *Oscar Wilde*, Weidenfeld & Nicolson, 1976

CRITICISM

Karl Beckson (ed.), *Oscar Wilde: The Critical Heritage*, Routledge and Kegan Paul, 1970

Sos Eltis, *Revising Wilde: Society and Subversion in the Plays of Oscar Wilde*, Oxford University Press, 1996

Regenia Gagnier, *Idylls of the Marketplace: Oscar Wilde and the Victorian Public*, Scolar Press, 1987

Regenia Gagnier, *Critical Essays on Oscar Wilde*, Macmillan, 1992

Joel H. Kaplan and Sheila Stowell, *Theatre and Fashion: Oscar Wilde to the Suffragettes*, Cambridge University Press, 1994

Christopher S. Nassaar, *Into the Demon Universe: A Literary Exploration of Oscar Wilde*, Yale University Press, 1974

Kerry Powell, *Oscar Wilde and the Theatre of the 1890s*, Cambridge University Press, 1990

Peter Raby, *Oscar Wilde*, Cambridge University Press, 1988

Neil Sammells, *Wilde Style: The Plays and Prose of Oscar Wilde*, Pearson Education, 2000

Alan Sinfield, *The Wilde Century: Effeminacy, Oscar Wilde and the Queer Moment*, Cassell, 1994

Katharine Worth, *Oscar Wilde*, Macmillan, 1987

GENERAL

William Archer, *Play-Making*, 1912 (reprinted 2006 by Dodo Press)

Neil Bartlett, *Who Was That Man? A Present for Mr Oscar Wilde*, Serpent's Tail, 1988

Laurel Brake, *Subjugated Knowledges: Journalism, Gender and Literature, 1837–1907*, Palgrave Macmillan, 1994

Judith Butler, *Gender Trouble: Feminism and the Subversion of Identity*, Routledge, 1990

Martin Esslin, *The Field of Drama: How the Signs of Drama Create Meaning on Stage and Screen*, Methuen, 1987

Ronald Hayman, *How to Read a Play*, Methuen, 1977

Julie Holledge, *Innocent Flowers: Women in the Edwardian Theatre*, Virago, 1981

H. Montgomery Hyde, *The Trials of Oscar Wilde*, William Hodge & Company, 1948

Russell Jackson, *Victorian Theatre: The Theatre in Its Time*, A & C Black, 1989

Declan Kiberd, *Inventing Ireland: The Literature of the Modern Nation*, Vintage, 1995

David Lavender, *The Penguin Book of the American West*, Penguin Books, 1965

Mary Luckhurst (ed.), *A Companion to Modern British and Irish Drama: 1880–2005*, Blackwell Publishing, 2006

Michael Mangan, *Staging Masculinities: History, Gender, Performance*, Palgrave Macmillan, 2002

Ellen Moers, *The Dandy: Brummell to Beerbohm*, University of Nebraska Press, 1978

Hesketh Pearson, *Beerbohm Tree: His Life and Laughter*, Methuen, 1956

Mary Poovey, *Uneven Developments: The Ideological Work of Gender in Mid-Victorian England*, University of Chicago Press, 1988

George Rowell (ed.), *Nineteenth Century Plays*, Oxford University Press, 1972

J. L. Styan, *Modern Drama in Theory and Practice: Realism and Naturalism*, Cambridge University Press, 1981

John Russell Taylor, *The Rise and Fall of the Well Made Play*, Methuen, 1967

Judith R. Walkowitz, *City of Dreadful Delight: Narratives of Sexual Danger in Late-Victorian London*, Virago, 1992

LITERARY TERMS

allusion a passing reference in a work of literature to something outside the text; may include other works of literature, myth, historical facts or biographical detail

ambiguous having the capacity to have double, multiple or uncertain meanings

aside when a character speaks in such a way that some or all of the other characters on the stage cannot hear what is being said; or they address the audience directly. It is a device used to reveal a character's private thoughts, emotions and intentions

body language how people show their feelings and emotions by the way they move, sit or stand – often revealing that these are different from those they are expressing in words

boulevard drama French plays of the early nineteenth century with intricate plots of sexual intrigue

cliché a widely used expression which, through overuse, has lost impact and originality

colloquial everyday speech used by people in informal situations

comedy story with a happy ending, most commonly, but not exclusively, used of plays

comedy of manners witty drama grounded in the battle of the sexes, in which the humour is chiefly verbal

crisis the moment in a play where the tension reaches a peak and a **resolution** is imminent. There may be one crisis or several crises, each one culminating in a climax

dandy man or woman who places great emphasis on personal style as a way of defying social conformity and rigid hierarchy

denouement point in the play where the whole plot has finally unfolded (from the French for 'unknotting')

development and complication central section of a **well-made play** which makes the situation more complex and creates **suspense** about the outcome

epigram pithy saying

eponymous adjective describing the character who gives his or her name to the title of a play or novel

exposition opening of a play in which all the information that the audience needs in order to understand the situation is put over. In a **well-made play** the playwright tries to do this without making the fact obvious

fourth wall naturalistic plays are often set in rooms; effectively, one 'wall' of these rooms is removed, allowing the audience to look in. Occasionally an actor might face the audience while looking into an imaginary mirror or fire, something that might be present on the 'wall'

hyperbole deliberate exaggeration, used for effect (from the Greek for 'throwing too far')

imagery descriptive language which uses images to make actions, objects and characters more vivid in the reader's mind. **Metaphors** and **similes** are examples of imagery

ingénue term for the innocent young heroine of the play; nineteenth- and early twentieth-century companies would employ an actress who specialised in such roles. See also **jeune premier**

irony incongruity between what might be expected and what actually happens; the ill-timed arrival of an event that had been hoped for

jeune premier young hero of the play, generally in love with the **ingénue**; sometimes also called the juvenile lead

melodrama popular theatrical genre of the nineteenth century. Distinguished by moralistic plots – often rooted in class struggle – with sensational effects. Music played an important role; originally it was used to evade the licensing laws which made it difficult for theatres to stage spoken drama, but it became important as a device to heighten the emotion of climactic moments

metaphor figure of speech in which a word or phrase is applied to an object, a character or an action which does not literally belong to it, in order to imply a resemblance and create an unusual or striking image

motivation desires and intentions that drive characters in **naturalistic** drama to behave as they do

music hall place of popular entertainment with singers and comedians; unlike characters in a **naturalistic** play, they interacted with the audience

narrative story, tale or any recital of events, and the manner in which it is told

naturalistic, naturalism theatrical style which tries to create the illusion of reality on the stage. The actors do not address the audience, but behave as if they are unaware of them; the language and situations are intended to be credible and realistic; and the settings mirror the real world as closely as possible

paradox seemingly absurd or self-contradictory statement that is or may be true

parody imitation of a work of literature or a literary style designed to ridicule the original

properties, props objects used in the play, some of which may be important to the action, such as Illingworth's glove in Act IV

proscenium arch arch which frames the opening between stage and audience in theatres built during the nineteenth or early twentieth centuries. It marks the edge of the **fourth wall**. In Wilde's time the frame extended round all four sides of this 'wall' like a picture frame, although the bottom border later disappeared. This form of stage is associated with **naturalism**

protagonist principal character in a work of literature

proviso scene a scene in which the heroine spells out to the hero the conditions under which she would be prepared to marry him. A feature of the **comedy of manners**, such scenes are generally comic in tone, although they also reflect some of the grimmer contemporary realities about marriage

realism the literary portrayal of the 'real' world, in both physical and psychological detail, rather than an imaginary or ideal one. Victorian novels sometimes described themselves in this way

resolution final moments of a play in which the loose ends are tied up

reversal of expectation scene which surprises the audience by changing the whole course of the story or the balance of sympathy in the play

rhetorical question one that expects the reply to indicate that one agrees with the questioner

Romantic related to the Romantic movement of the late eighteenth century and early nineteenth century that idealised nature

satire type of literature in which folly, evil or topical issues are held up to scorn through ridicule, **irony** or exaggeration

scène à faire term invented by French pioneers of the **well-made play** to indicate a crucial scene, usually a confrontation, which the audience would anticipate with excitement

simile figure of speech which compares two things using the words 'like' or 'as'

soliloquy a dramatic device which allows a character to speak directly to the audience as if thinking aloud, revealing their inner thoughts, feelings and intentions

stage business non-verbal action on the stage, prescribed in the stage directions or added by actor or director

stock character the kind of character one could expect to see in a particular genre – for example the oppressed mother in a **melodrama**; the 'best friend' who listens to the confidences of the hero or heroine in a romantic **comedy**; the gossipy old woman who exists mainly to relay information to the audience in a **naturalistic** play

strong curtain a powerful line of dialogue or situation which occurs just before the curtain fall. Generally placed immediately before the last act to maximise **suspense** about the outcome

subtext theatrical term to describe a pattern of emotions and energies that are not directly spoken about but show themselves through trivial actions or remarks which seem casual on the surface. It is a feature of **naturalistic** drama and Wilde was a pioneer of the technique in England

suspense excitement about the outcome of the story, often raised to a high pitch just before a break in the action

symbolic, symbolism investing material objects with abstract powers and meanings greater than their own; allowing a complex idea to be represented by a single object

tableau if the situation at the end of an act was particularly striking, Victorian actors would briefly 'freeze' to allow the audience to take in the stage picture

tragedy in its original sense, a drama dealing with elevated actions and emotions and characters of high social standing in which a terrible outcome becomes inevitable as a result of an unstoppable sequence of events and a fatal flaw in the personality of the **protagonist**. More recently, tragedy has come to include courses of events happening to ordinary individuals that are inevitable because of social and cultural conditions or natural disasters

well-made play the form taken by most Victorian West End drama, derived from the French dramatists Scribe and Sardou. A well-made play has a clear structure: the **exposition** tells us what we need to know (usually that some of the characters have a secret); the **development and complication** bring the situation to **crisis** point, usually around the end of the penultimate act, as secrets come out and throw people into confusion; finally there is a **resolution**

Frances Gray is Reader in Drama at the University of Sheffield. She has written widely on theatre: her published books include titles on Noël Coward and women in the theatre. She is also a playwright, and has a Radio Times award for comedy.

NOTES

GCSE

Maya Angelou
I Know Why the Caged Bird Sings

Jane Austen
Pride and Prejudice

Alan Ayckbourn
Absent Friends

Elizabeth Barrett Browning
Selected Poems

Robert Bolt
A Man for All Seasons

Harold Brighouse
Hobson's Choice

Charlotte Brontë
Jane Eyre

Emily Brontë
Wuthering Heights

Brian Clark
Whose Life is it Anyway?

Robert Cormier
Heroes

Shelagh Delaney
A Taste of Honey

Charles Dickens
David Copperfield
Great Expectations
Hard Times
Oliver Twist
Selected Stories

Roddy Doyle
Paddy Clarke Ha Ha Ha

George Eliot
Silas Marner
The Mill on the Floss

Anne Frank
The Diary of a Young Girl

William Golding
Lord of the Flies

Oliver Goldsmith
She Stoops to Conquer

Willis Hall
The Long and the Short and the Tall

Thomas Hardy
Far from the Madding Crowd
The Mayor of Casterbridge
Tess of the d'Urbervilles
The Withered Arm and other Wessex Tales

L. P. Hartley
The Go-Between

Seamus Heaney
Selected Poems

Susan Hill
I'm the King of the Castle

Barry Hines
A Kestrel for a Knave

Louise Lawrence
Children of the Dust

Harper Lee
To Kill a Mockingbird

Laurie Lee
Cider with Rosie

Arthur Miller
The Crucible
A View from the Bridge

Robert O'Brien
Z for Zachariah

Frank O'Connor
My Oedipus Complex and Other Stories

George Orwell
Animal Farm

J. B. Priestley
An Inspector Calls
When We Are Married

Willy Russell
Educating Rita
Our Day Out

J. D. Salinger
The Catcher in the Rye

William Shakespeare
Henry IV Part I
Henry V
Julius Caesar
Macbeth
The Merchant of Venice
A Midsummer Night's Dream
Much Ado About Nothing
Romeo and Juliet
The Tempest
Twelfth Night

George Bernard Shaw
Pygmalion

Mary Shelley
Frankenstein

R. C. Sherriff
Journey's End

Rukshana Smith
Salt on the Snow

John Steinbeck
Of Mice and Men

Robert Louis Stevenson
Dr Jekyll and Mr Hyde

Jonathan Swift
Gulliver's Travels

Robert Swindells
Daz 4 Zoe

Mildred D. Taylor
Roll of Thunder, Hear My Cry

Mark Twain
Huckleberry Finn

James Watson
Talking in Whispers

Edith Wharton
Ethan Frome

William Wordsworth
Selected Poems

A Choice of Poets

Mystery Stories of the Nineteenth Century including The Signalman

Nineteenth Century Short Stories

Poetry of the First World War

Six Women Poets

For the AQA Anthology:

Duffy and Armitage & Pre-1914 Poetry

Heaney and Clarke & Pre-1914 Poetry

Poems from Different Cultures

Key Stage 3

William Shakespeare
Henry V
Macbeth
Much Ado About Nothing
Richard III
The Tempest

Margaret Atwood
Cat's Eye
The Handmaid's Tale

Jane Austen
Emma
Mansfield Park
Persuasion
Pride and Prejudice
Sense and Sensibility

William Blake
Songs of Innocence and of Experience

Charlotte Brontë
Jane Eyre
Villette

Emily Brontë
Wuthering Heights

Angela Carter
Nights at the Circus
Wise Children

Geoffrey Chaucer
The Franklin's Prologue and Tale
The Merchant's Prologue and Tale
The Miller's Prologue and Tale
The Prologue to the Canterbury Tales
The Wife of Bath's Prologue and Tale

Samuel Coleridge
Selected Poems

Joseph Conrad
Heart of Darkness

Daniel Defoe
Moll Flanders

Charles Dickens
Bleak House
Great Expectations
Hard Times

Emily Dickinson
Selected Poems

John Donne
Selected Poems

Carol Ann Duffy
Selected Poems
The World's Wife

George Eliot
Middlemarch
The Mill on the Floss

T. S. Eliot
Selected Poems
The Waste Land

F. Scott Fitzgerald
The Great Gatsby

John Ford
'Tis Pity She's a Whore

E. M. Forster
A Passage to India

Michael Frayn
Spies

Charles Frazier
Cold Mountain

Brian Friel
Making History
Translations

William Golding
The Spire

Thomas Hardy
Jude the Obscure
The Mayor of Casterbridge
The Return of the Native
Selected Poems
Tess of the d'Urbervilles

Seamus Heaney
Selected Poems from 'Opened Ground'

Nathaniel Hawthorne
The Scarlet Letter

Homer
The Iliad
The Odyssey

Aldous Huxley
Brave New World

Kazuo Ishiguro
The Remains of the Day

Ben Jonson
The Alchemist

James Joyce
Dubliners

John Keats
Selected Poems

Philip Larkin
High Windows
The Whitsun Weddings and Selected Poems

Ian McEwan
Atonement

Christopher Marlowe
Doctor Faustus
Edward II

Arthur Miller
All My Sons
Death of a Salesman

John Milton
Paradise Lost Books I & II

Toni Morrison
Beloved

George Orwell
Nineteen Eighty-Four

Sylvia Plath
Selected Poems

William Shakespeare
Antony and Cleopatra
As You Like It
Hamlet
Henry IV Part I
King Lear
Macbeth
Measure for Measure
The Merchant of Venice
A Midsummer Night's Dream
Much Ado About Nothing
Othello
Richard II
Richard III
Romeo and Juliet
The Taming of the Shrew
The Tempest
Twelfth Night
The Winter's Tale

Mary Shelley
Frankenstein

Richard Brinsley Sheridan
The School for Scandal

Bram Stoker
Dracula

Jonathan Swift
Gulliver's Travels and A Modest Proposal

Alfred Tennyson
Selected Poems

Alice Walker
The Color Purple

Oscar Wilde
The Importance of Being Earnest
A Woman of No Importance

Tennessee Williams
Cat on a Hot Tin Roof
The Glass Menagerie
A Streetcar Named Desire

Jeanette Winterson
Oranges Are Not the Only Fruit

John Webster
The Duchess of Malfi

Virginia Woolf
To the Lighthouse

William Wordsworth
The Prelude and Selected Poems

W. B. Yeats
Selected Poems